D1599985

*Contemporary American Novelists
of the Absurd*

CONTEMPORARY AMERICAN NOVELISTS OF THE ABSURD

by

Charles B. Harris

COLLEGE & UNIVERSITY PRESS · *Publishers*

NEW HAVEN, CONN.

60935

MANUFACTURED IN THE UNITED STATES OF AMERICA BY
UNITED PRINTING SERVICES, INC.
NEW HAVEN, CONN.

To Vicki

Preface

The belief that ours is an absurd universe, chaotic and without meaning, is perhaps the dominant theme of the modern American novel. In presenting this theme, American novelists have generally employed conventional novelistic methods. That is, they have not followed the example of European novelists like Beckett and Robbe-Grillet who abandoned the traditional novel for more experimental forms. Near the end of the fifties and throughout the decade of the sixties, however, certain American novelists began presenting their vision of an absurd universe in new and different ways. Although these writers have managed to depart from the conventional novel, they do so without adopting an "anti-style" as an alternative. Rather, they continue employing traditional novelistic devices, but they employ them ironically, even farcically. Relying primarily upon the use of burlesque and parody, contemporary American novelists of the absurd mock the conventional novel as obsolete while simultaneously employing its conventions in vitally new ways.

Thus these novelists treat absurdist themes with what we may call absurdist techniques. Their vision of an absurd universe not only constitutes the theme of their novels but is reflected as well by the ways they manage incident, characterization, and language. This fusion of form and content becomes a kind of metaphor for their concerns. The result represents a significant innovation in the development of the American novel.

I have chosen for close examination four novelists representative of this trend: Joseph Heller, Kurt Vonnegut, Jr., Thomas Pynchon, and John Barth. The selection of these particular writers rests primarily on my belief that they have produced some of the most significant absurdist novels written in America today. This belief is guided in part by the large amount of critical attention already given them. With the exception of Vonnegut, who has been curiously ignored by critics, these writers have been the subject of more than fifty articles in professional journals, not to mention chapters in several books and hundreds of review articles. Few other novelists of the sixties have yet received such extensive critical attention or met with as much critical favor.

While the ages of these four novelists vary widely, all of their important novels were published during the sixties. Vonnegut, the oldest, was born in 1922. Heller and Barth were born in 1923 and 1930 respectively. Pynchon, the youngest, was born in 1937. Yet of the thirteen novels they have published so far, only four were published before 1960 and one of these in 1959. Generally, it is not until the sixties that those traits begin to appear which distinguish these writers from other American novelists who present a vision of absurdity in more conventional forms.

I have tried to give equal emphasis to the particular nature of each novelist's absurdist vision and to the methods he employs in presenting that vision. Because each novelist employs many of the same devices, I have focused attention in each chapter upon only the main device or devices used by the novelist discussed in that chapter. In discussing Heller's *Catch-22*, for example, I examine the use of burlesque, language, and structure as they reinforce the absurdist vision in that novel. In the chapter concerning Vonnegut, on the other hand, I discuss his use of tone and two-dimensional characters. In Chapter Four, I consider

Pynchon's use of entropy and, to a lesser extent, the Quantum Theory as controlling metaphors; and in Chapter Five I examine the novels of John Barth as "inverted paradigms." It is my hope that such selectivity avoids redundancy and allows a more intensive study of the various absurdist methods under consideration.

In the final chapter of this study, I consider Camp and pop-art as extensions of the absurdist method. The arguments of certain prominent critics that the novel has ceased to exist as a viable form necessitates this discussion. Susan Sontag, Norman Mailer and Leslie Fiedler, among others, insist that Camp and the pop-novel have usurped the role of the novel in modern society. In expressing my disagreement with the "death-of-art" critics, who I feel have misunderstood the true nature of Camp and the pop-novel, I also discuss a number of other absurdist novels, including some by younger, less well-known writers.

I have tried in this study to explore the attitudes of certain contemporary American novelists of the absurd, to analyze some of the reasons they have felt compelled to discover new methods for presenting a sense of absurdity, which is rather different from mere thematic concern with the subject, and to examine some of these methods of presentation. I have restricted the concerns of the study to the American novel only, although the attitudes and methods I discuss are not necessarily confined to America. Indeed, in the works of the Argentine novelist Jorge Luis Borges and especially of that Russian writer "turned" American, Vladimir Nabokov, these attitudes and methods are quite predominant. Similarly, I have focused only upon those novels first published in or near the decade of the sixties. Isolated examples of novels displaying the treatment of absurdist themes with absurdist techniques may be found earlier than the sixties, particularly the novels of Nathanael West, who in many ways is the "father" of the contemporary absurdist novel. But the first recognition of the critical importance of this novelistic development belongs to the sixties. Never before has such an abundance of absurdist novels appeared in so short a time. Indeed, the practice of treating absurdist themes with absurdist techniques becomes almost standard during the sixties, a period that can rightfully be called the Decade of the Absurd.

Acknowledgments

I gratefully acknowledge my indebtedness to Professor Paul Hurley who guided this study from its inception and whose learning and good taste rescued me from a multitude of intellectual pitfalls. I am also grateful to Professors Howard Webb, James Benziger, John Howell, Archibald McLeod and Larry E. Taylor, each of whom read the entire manuscript and offered many helpful suggestions. For permission to quote from copyrighted material, I am indebted to Simon and Schuster for passages from Joseph Heller's *Catch-22*, copyrighted © 1955 by Joseph Heller. Finally, I extend my deepest gratitude to my wife Vicki, without whose patience and encouragement this study would not have been possible.

C. B. H.

Contents

Contemporary American Novelists
of the Absurd

I

The Aesthetics of Absurdity

THE ABSURDIST VISION may be defined as the belief that we are trapped in a meaningless universe and that neither God nor man, theology nor philosophy, can make sense of the human condition. The expression of this vision in literature is hardly confined to the twentieth century. Yet never before has the notion of absurdity found corroboration in so many extra-literary areas. The "new" logic, with its acceptance of the illogical, and modern science, with its denial of causality and its concept of entropy, elevate chaos to the level of scientific fact. Recent sociological tracts argue convincingly that we are a lonely crowd of organization men, growing up absurd. Modern existential philosophy warns that we face a loss of self in a fragmented world of technology that reduces man to the operational and functional.[1] Each of these theories seems to lend support to what certain writers have believed for a long time, that ours is a disintegrating world without a unifying principle, without meaning, without purpose: an absurd universe.

Even the workaday citizen, non-conversant with such "philosophical" or "technical" matters, is not unaware that ours is an age of distress. In the last decade alone he has witnessed from the comfort of his own living room televised film clips of combat in Viet Nam, the actual slaying of a presidential assassin (repeated in slow motion!), a racial riot in Watts, and a "police riot" in Chicago. A

17

streamlined news media has kept him in touch with such extreme and volatile personalities as Timothy Leary and H. L. Hunt, George Lincoln Rockwell and Malcolm X, Spiro Agnew and George Wallace, Mayor Daley and Abbie Hoffman. Indeed, the term *modern* itself—in Irving Howe's definition—"as it refers to both history and literature, signifies extreme situations and radical solutions. It summons images of war and revolution, experiment and disaster, apocalypse and skepticism; images of rebellion, disenchantment, and nothingness."[2]

The contemporary American novelist who chooses absurdity as his theme must treat that theme in an age when Nietzsche's agonizing cry that "God is dead!" can be found scrawled upon the graffiti-covered walls of public lavatories, and when the vocabulary of existential anxiety, like the vocabulary of Freudian psychology, has become part of undergraduate cant. He must, in short, write in an age when absurdity, because it is taken for granted, is no longer taken seriously.

Philip Roth comments on this dilemma in an article entitled "Writing American Fiction." After describing at great length the gruesome yet comic details surrounding a Chicago murder, Roth concludes:

> And what is the moral of so long a story? Simply this: that the American writer in the middle of the twentieth century has his hands full in trying to understand, and then describe, and then make *credible* much of the American reality. It stupifies, it sickens, it infuriates, and finally it is even a kind of embarrassment to one's own meager imagination. The actuality is continually outdoing our talents, and the culture tosses up figures almost daily that are the envy of any novelist.[3]

Burton Feldman joins Roth in believing the contemporary novelist's imagination has not kept pace with an absurd age. Their "humor isn't audacious enough for a world like ours," he complains of the so-called black humor novelists. "The ordinary reader will find that he can trump the nihilism or apocalypse of these novels in a twinkling. . . . Such a reader can only be agreed with if he concludes that the world is surely worse than Black Humor is telling him."[4]

In fact, fantasy, which long seemed the exclusive prov-
ince of art, everyday intrudes itself into the world of reality. There exists, says Bruce Jay Friedman in his introduction to *Black Humor*, "a fading line between fantasy and
reality, a very fading line." To write comic fantasy today,
he suggests, all one need do is report, journalistically, the
current scene. Sounding a lot like Roth and Feldman,
Friedman complains that the novelist's role as social satirist
has been unconsciously usurped by the news media:

> The journalist who, in 1964, must cover the ecumenical debate
> on whether the Jews, on the one hand, are still to be known as
> Christ-killers, or, on the other hand, are to be let off the hook,
> is certainly today's satirist. The novelist-satirist, with no real
> territory to roam, has had to discover new land, invent a new
> currency, a new set of filters, has had to sail into darker waters
> somewhere out beyond satire. . . .[5]

John Aldridge agrees upon the necessity for discovering
"a new set of filters." "The task of the novelist in a time
like ours," he writes, "can no longer be confined to a
simple exploration of the social appearances and surfaces,
but must be expanded and deepened to take into account
the chaotic multiplicity of meaning; which now confront us
both above and beneath the surfaces." Yet, Aldridge continues, "to deal effectively with the mass complications and
ambiguities . . . to say nothing of the present amorphous
state of American society, a writer would ideally need the
artistic equipment of an Orwell, a Kafka, Camus, Celine, or
Dostoevsky."[6] What has been called "realistic portraiture"[7] —and this includes stream-of-consciousness novels,
which constitute a kind of psychic realism—is a method no
longer viable in our modern age. In other words, if contemporary novelists are to portray absurdity effectively in a
world which already accepts absurdity as a basic premise,
an everyday fact, they must find new ways to present their
vision.

Recent American novelists of the absurd have responded
to this challenge. Verifying this assumption are the repeated
attempts of certain critics in the past decade to subsume
the novels of the sixties under some general critical head-

ing. "Black Humor," "black comedy," "affluent terrorism," "Epicurean comedy," "the psychic novel," "the novel of disintegration"—all of these have been recently offered as congeneric tagnames.[8] Such an effort by critics suggests that something innovative, perhaps even a new movement in American literature, is indeed afoot. Now a concern with absurdity is not, as students of American literature are aware, new to the American novel. The novels of Melville, the later Twain, West, Hemingway and the early Faulkner, not to mention those novels of the fifties discussed by Ihab Hassan and Richard Lehan in their excellent examinations of the existential novel in America,[9] all reflect a belief that the world is disjointed, purposeless, absurd. New to the novels of the sixties, however, is the particular treatment of absurdist themes. It is to that interesting subject that we must now turn.

An analogue to recent developments in the American novel may be found in the Theater of the Absurd in France. The basic distinction between the Existential theater of Sartre and Camus and the Theater of the Absurd— that of Beckett, Ionesco, and Genet—is, as Martin Esslin contends, that the former presents absurdity in a "form of highly lucid and logically constructed reasoning," whereas the latter "strives to express its sense of the senselessness of the human condition and the inadequacy of the rational approach by the open abandonment of rational devices and discursive thought."[10] As we shall see, the absurdist novel of the sixties in America is rarely so total in its commitment to absurdity as are the French plays nor does it completely abandon the use of "rational devices." But its basic distinction from the novels preceding it—which also often maintain absurdist themes—is that the absurdist novel of the sixties, like the French Theater of the Absurd, seeks new ways to integrate subject matter and form.

This is not to say that the novelists covered in this study form part of a self-conscious school or movement. The differences between John Barth and Thomas Pynchon or Joseph Heller and Kurt Vonnegut, Jr., are obvious to most readers. Each of these novelists takes a distinctive approach to both subject matter and form. Yet it is also clear that they share certain innovative characteristics. What is new about these novelists, as Richard Kostelanetz has noted, is their fusion of an "absurd base," or subject matter, with an "absurd surface," or form.[11] Such a fusion, for reasons to be discussed later, is seldom maintained throughout the entirety of any single absurdist novel, and its use is more extensive in some novels than in others. But in almost every novel published by these writers after 1960, the vision of an absurd world not only constitutes the novel's theme but is reflected as well by incident, characterization, and language.

It must be stressed that what I have in mind here is not merely that form reflects content. Such unity forms an organic part of most successful novels. But with one or two exceptions—Melville's *The Confidence Man* and the novels of Nathanael West come to mind—never before in an American novel has the concept of absurdity been actually revealed through form.

My point can be explained by reference to Hemingway's *The Sun Also Rises*. The purposelessness and lack of meaning in the hollow lives of the characters in that novel is certainly emphasized by the novel's circular structure. "Nothing leads anywhere in the book" writes Philip Young, "and that is perhaps the real point of it. The action comes full circle—imitates, that is, the sun of the title, which also rises, only to hasten to the place where it arose. . . ."[12] Similarly, as Young also points out, the language of Hemingway's novel reflects its theme: "the economy and narrow focus of the prose controls the little that can be absolutely mastered. The prose is tense because the atmosphere in which the struggle for control takes place is tense, and the tension in the style expresses that fact."[13] Nonetheless, even though Hemingway's use of form does help define his absurdist vision, the form is not itself absurd. The incidents are credible, not fantastic, and the description is realistic. The use of language, though distinctive, is unobtrusive. In other words, Hemingway made use of "rational devices and discursive thought" in his novel.

In the absurdist novels of the sixties, on the other hand, the ultimate absurdity of life is suggested by a series of preposterous and ridiculous events, by characters who—although described with apparent gravity—are distorted, exaggerated and caricatured, and by language which makes use of, to use Eugene McNamara's list, "lexical distortions, meaningless puns, and insistent repetition of empty words, clichés, exaggeration, and deliberately misplaced particulars, and juxtaposed incongruous details."[14] In other words, absurdity in these novels is revealed primarily through the device of comic exaggeration—in a word, burlesque.

Some of the reasons for—and uses of—burlesque in the contemporary novel have been discussed by John Barth in his article, "The Literature of Exhaustion." Barth refers to Jorge Luis Borges's idea that as far as fictional forms are concerned, "literary history . . . has pretty well exhausted the possibilities of novelty." Consequently, Barth continues, "for one to attempt to add overtly to the sum of 'original' literature by even so much as a conventional short story, not to mention a novel, would be too presumptuous, too naive; literature has been done long since."[15] The serious writer who accepts this point of view faces a creative *cul de sac* and might cease writing altogether. Such a silence, says Barth, would itself be "fairly meaningful" and is perhaps the direction now being taken by Beckett, whom Barth considers a "technically up-to-date artist." The silence of Beckett would then stand as a metaphor of sorts for the "silence *Molloy* speaks of, 'of which the universe is made.' "[16]

The charge that art forms are exhausted began as early as the Renaissance. Such charges are repeatedly disproven, however, and artistic conventions are constantly replaced by breakthroughs unimagined by prior generations of artists. Yet Barth's essay is not a dirge sung over the bier of narrative literature. Rather, it offers a suggestion for a new and original direction that the novel might take. Barth's most significant thought is that, instead of silence, the novelist can continue to employ the "exhausted" forms of the past, but he must employ them ironically. If Beethoven's Sixth were composed today, for instance, it would be an embarrassment unless, as Barth maintains, it were "done with ironic intent by a composer quite aware of where we've been and where we are." In this case, the work would make an "ironic comment ... on the genre and history of the art. ... "[17] Even though the form would still be identical to the original, the effect, the ultimate meaning, and therefore the work itself, would be new and different. By consciously imitating a form the possibilities of which are seemingly exhausted and employing it against itself, the composer could produce "new Human work."[18]

Burlesque allows American novelists of the absurd to reject traditional forms and styles while at the same time continuing to use these forms and styles. Consequently, they seldom employ what Leslie Fiedler calls "the fallacy of imitative form" by attempting to reproduce absurdity through an "anti-style."[19] In a way, such "imitation" is what is happening in the French Theater of the Absurd and the *nouveau roman*, both of which may be seen as attempts to reproduce that absurdity felt by the artists to lie just beneath the surface of existence.[20] American novelists of the absurd, on the other hand, while they sometimes exaggerate "reality," seldom feel the need to distort it beyond recognition.[21] In fact, they usually don't imitate "life" at all, but other novels, other forms, other styles. Yet their imitation, because ironic, transcends mere mimesis and becomes a comment upon the artificiality not only of art, but of life as it is usually lived, of mass society, and of all things which prevent the realization that life is absurd. This is what Barth is talking about when he says, "A different way to come to terms with the discrepancy between art and the Real Thing is to *affirm* the artificial element in art (you can't get rid of it anyway), and make the artifice part of your point. ... "[22] The artifice is of course emphasized by exaggeration: the plots are often a little too elaborately structured and involve a few too many coincidences; the incidents are often fantastic, far beyond the pale of verisimilitude; the language is often florid, comically pyrotechnic. At the same time, when the burlesque is temporarily suspended, what often emerges is beautifully rendered prose; prose, it might be added, that is grammatical, conventionally punctuated and written in sentences that, though highly elaborate, are conventionally structured—a lack of linguistic iconoclasm rare to the American novel since James. Gifted stylists, these novelists can skillfully manipulate the conventions of prose. If they choose instead to burlesque these conventions it is because they believe them appropriate to times less complex than ours. Their use of burlesque, then, allows the novelists of the absurd to utilize all the traditional conventions of characterization, language, and plot while at the same time expressing their distrust of these and similar conventions. Thus they are able, in Barth's words, to "[throw] out the bath water without for a moment losing the baby."[23]

In their ironic use of traditional forms and styles, the contemporary novelists of the absurd often turn to parody, a salient characteristic of many of their novels. Barth's *The Sot-Weed Factor*, for example, has been called a mock-epic, a parody of the picaresque novel, and is certainly a burlesque of the historical and biographical novel; his *Giles Goat-Boy* can be read as a parody of the Bible. Heller's *Catch-22* and James Purdy's *Malcolm* have been called American Romance parodies. *Malcolm* and Donald Barthelme's *Snow White* parody the fairy tale, and several of Vonnegut's novels, expecially *Sirens of Titan* and *Slaughterhouse-Five*, may be viewed as parodies of science fiction and Utopian fantasy. Thomas Berger's *Little Big Man* mocks the Western. *Giles Goat-Boy* and Vonnegut's *Mother Night* masquerade as other works which have been "discovered" or "edited" by the novelist and then "presented" to the reader. Moreover, Barth parodies the complete text of *Oedipus Rex* in *Giles Goat-Boy*, and Pynchon parodies at length a Jacobean tragedy in *The Crying of Lot-49*. Barth's *The Sot-Weed Factor* and Vonnegut's *The Sirens of Titan* contain parodies of historical documents, and parodies of poems and modern song lyrics are sprinkled throughout the novels by these writers.[24]

Now parody and burlesque hardly represent innovations

in the novel. Indeed, these devices were among the first used by novelists, as such famous parodies as *Shamela* and *Joseph Andrews* attest. Contemporary novelists of the absurd have discovered new ways to use these traditional devices, however. Burlesque in their novels is not only directed toward the external world but, as Robert Buckeye points out, often becomes "reflexive in nature. ... It is an irony toward [the novelist] as author, the value of art, the possibility of language,"[25] What the contemporary novelists of the absurd wish both to ridicule and place in proper perspective is literature itself—or at least the traditional view of literature.

Literature in general, and the novel in particular, has traditionally been seen as a way of ordering reality. The novelist takes something not aesthetic, life, and gives it shape, form, congruity. Even if his theme is the incongruity of an absurd universe—as in the novels of Hemingway or Camus—his treatment of this theme involves a coherent structure; that is, he orders his materials in an "artistic" way. It is true that the traditional aim of novelists is to make their artistic creation appear to be life, yet—because they artistically shape reality—what is ultimately presented is something unlike reality, or at least unlike reality as it is conceived of in the twentieth century.[26] The reflexive use of burlesque and parody, on the other hand, provides contemporary absurdist novelists a method for rejecting literary pretensions to comprehend and order reality or any part of reality. Thus these writers burlesque not only life but the very vehicle they employ to examine life. This ridicule is by no means confined to literature but is also directed toward history (especially in *The Sot-Weed Factor*, *V.*, *The Crying of Lot-49* and *Little Big Man*), religion (especially in *Cat's Cradle*, *The Sirens of Titan*, and *Giles Goat-Boy*) and philosophy (especially Barth's novels), all of which try to impose some direction or order or meaning upon existence.

Life, these novelists believe, resists any impositions of order because its realities are multiple. Any attempt to order these multiple meanings, unless done ironically, results in a falsification of reality. This view of a multiple reality reflects the influence of Einsteinian relativity and quantum physics. The Quantum Theory, as defined by Richard Kostelanetz, maintains that "experience that is discontinuous defies precise definition—its direction is indeterminate; and phenomena that have a semblance of meaning turn out, upon closer inspection, to suggest a multiplicity of answers."[27] Symbols for this multiplicity abound in the contemporary absurdist novels. The multiple v's in Pynchon's *V.*, the multiple identities of Fausto in that same novel, of Henry Burlingame in Barth's *The Sot-Weed Factor*, and of Harold Bray in *Giles Goat-Boy*, the doubt cast upon whether or not characters like Doc Daneeka in Heller's *Catch—22*, Malcolm in Purdy's *Malcolm*, and Jacob Horner in Barth's *The End of the Road* even have identities—each of these suggests that truth is not ambiguous, but multiple; that it is not merely elusive, but, as quantum physics tells us, by its very existence uncertain.

In a world such as this, in which there is no reality but only realities, "what better way to represent it," asks Buckeye, "than [by] parody: to present a reality that is questioned by another. . . ."[28] Parody not only ridicules the pretensions of literature (or history or philosophy or religion) to understand life but rejects as well the view of an ordered universe reflected in the art form being parodied.[29] Moreover, by turning art back upon itself, by confronting what Barth calls "an intellectual dead end and employing it against itself,"[30] the novelist achieves a viable art form, its "newness" lying paradoxically in its very "oldness."

Not only traditional forms, but fictional characters as well, are burlesqued in the contemporary novel of the absurd. Both Eugene McNamara and Leslie Fiedler have commented on the resemblance of figures in recent absurdist novels to comic strip characters.[31] Not only their "occasional obviousness and thinness of texture,"[32] but their very names—Dr. Hilarius, Chief White Halfoat, and Billy Pilgrim, for example—suggest the types of names given cartoon figures—Daddy Warbucks, Jughead, Flat-top, etc. As in comic strips, the names often suggest specific attitudes or ideas. Dr. Hilarius is an inept psychiatrist in *The Crying of*

Lot-49. Billy Pilgrim makes extraterrestrial pilgrimages in Vonnegut's *Slaughterhouse-Five.* *Giles Goat-Boy* contains a scientist named Eierkopf (egg-head) and the overseer of a gigantic furnace room named Maurice Stoker. Scatology abounds: Heller gives us a Lieutenant Scheisskopf, and Pynchon creates a Scheissvogel (in *V.*). Mike Fallopian is a character in *The Crying of Lot-49*, and Harry Pena is a virile fisherman in *God Bless You, Mr. Rosewater.* Even when these names don't directly suggest an attitude, they are comic and obviously not "realistic." In *The Sot-Weed Factor*, Ebeneezer Cook meets an Indian chief named Kekataughtassapooekskumoughmass. Pynchon's novels offer characters like Stanley Koteks, Diocletian Blobb, and Genghis Cohen (*Crying of Lot-49*) and Benny Profane, Bloody Chiclitz, and Winsome, Charisma, and Fu (*V.*). In *God Bless You, Mr. Rosewater*, Vonnegut portrays a sixty-eight-year-old virgin named Diana Moon Glampers, and in *Cat's Cradle* he names a doctor after an organ stop, Dr. Vox Humana. One of Barth's Indians is called Drakepecker.

Contemporary novelists of the absurd did not invent two-dimensional characters or comic names. But they use these devices for new reasons. The use of two-dimensional characters affords these writers one way to emphasize the artificiality of art, which, as we have seen, is one of their aims. Their use of caricature also indicates their rejection of the assumption underlying realistic characterization that human beings can be accurately formulated. As aspects of a protean reality, human beings remain as illusive and as problematic as the absurd universe they occupy. By over-simplifying their characters in an exaggerated way, contemporary novelists of the absurd suggest the complexity of human nature by indirection.

Another effect of the use of two-dimensional, "comic-strip" characters is that normal processes of life and death, not to mention of pain and sorrow, are temporarily suspended. Aesthetically detached and objective, we can only laugh when a cartoon coyote is tricked into falling down a canyon by a cartoon roadrunner. Similarly, we remain detached from the often flat, two-dimensional, and unreal

characters in the contemporary absurdist novels. Our dis-
engagement, in fact, explains much of the so-called black
humor of these novels. Often we find ourselves laughing at
the various cruel and violent events that fill their pages.

What separates these works from usual comic novels is
that we are not allowed to maintain the objectivity which
permits emotional distance. Realistic incidents frequently
intrude upon the fantastic and grotesque. We may be able
to laugh at the various attempts made upon Yossarian's life
by Nately's whore in Heller's *Catch-22*, and we may giggle
at the numerous collisions with inanimate objects encoun-
tered by Benny Profane in Pynchon's *V.*. But we can only
be shocked and appalled at the death of Snowden in *Catch-
22*, described by Heller in gory detail, and at the graphic
description of Esther Harvitz's "nose-job" in *V.* These passages are as realistic as any found in those novels Paul
Levine classifies as "neo-realistic."[33] Indeed, violent and
grotesque events such as these are often presented in a
calm, precise, and logical prose style. Rather than reflect
absurdity, such treatment seems in conflict with the absurdity being presented.

The combination of fantastic events with realistic presentation results in reader disorientation. The reader is faced
with a situation comparable to that of Chief Bromden's in
Ken Kesey's absurdist *One Flew Over the Cuckoo's Nest*.
Bromden sees the world as being "like a cartoon world,
where the figures are flat and outlined in black, jerking
through some kind of goofy story that might be real funny
if it weren't for the cartoon figures being real guys. . . ."[34]
Accustomed to the mimetic tradition in the novel, the
reader—upon first confronting the fantastic and cartoon-like
surface of these absurdist novels—must adjust his expectations. However, as Eugene McNamara points out, "once the
reader has adjusted his imagination to the demand of
tran[s]ferrial [*sic*] comic strip or cartoon attitudes to the
medium of fiction, he is upset again by a return to a more
serious traditional attitude."[35] Confusion results, but it is
calculated confusion, for the novelist is attempting to evoke
in the reader some response to the idea of absurdity. It is

as if the novelist is saying, "You may have adjusted to your own absurd world, but it will be more difficult to adjust to the absurdity in the world of my novel." The desired result is similar to the purpose attributed by Esslin to the French Theater of the Absurd.

> Human beings [he writes], who in their daily lives confront a world that has split up into a series of disconnected fragments and lost its purpose, but who are no longer aware of this state of affairs and its disintegrating effect on their personalities, are brought face to face with a heightened representation of this schizophrenic universe. ... And this, in turn, results in the liberating effect of anxieties overcome by being formulated. This is the nature of all the gallows humor and the *humour noir* of world literature, of which the Theatre of the Absurd is the latest example.[36]

The burlesque of plot, characterization and language, which includes the combination of realistic and fantastic modes, is designed, as we have seen, to evoke in the reader a response to the absurd. Although the reader lives in an absurd universe and may even accept its absurdity, his acceptance is academic. He has become inured to absurdity. To present this absurdity in traditionally naturalistic terms only would affect the reader little if at all.[37] But by an ironic exploitation of traditional forms as well as by skillful manipulation of burlesque and naturalistic modes, the novelist achieves a form that is both original and efficacious.

So even though contemporary absurdist novelists mock literature, they have some faith in its efficacy. As Robert Scholes points out, however, theirs is not the faith of the traditional satirist, who hopes to reform society through ridicule and invective, nor of the traditional writer of comedy, who hopes to better mankind by exposing folly and wickedness, although many traditional satiric and comic techniques do appear in their novels.[38] Moreover, although the problems and conflicts of tragedy often appear in these novels, the novelists lack the traditional faith of the tragedian, who believes that though man may fall, the absolute, an ordered universe, lies beyond destruction. "In the final instance," writes Jan Kott, "tragedy is an appraisal of human fate, a measure of the absolute."[39] In the twentieth century, however, no belief in absolutes exists; not only is man out of joint, but so is his universe. Instead of tragedy, therefore, we have the grotesque.

> In the world of the grotesque [writes Kott], downfall cannot be justified by, or blamed on, the absolute. The absolute is not endowed with any ultimate reasons; it is stronger, and that is all. *The absolute is absurd.* . . . Various kinds of impersonal and hostile mechanisms have taken the place of God, Nature, and History, found in the old tragedy. The notion of absurd mechanism is probably the last metaphysical concept remaining in modern grotesque. But this absurd mechanism is not transcendental any more in relation to . . . mankind.[40]

Comedy inheres in the grotesque, for "the absence of tragedy in a tragic world," Kott quotes Maurice Regnault as saying, "gives birth to comedy."[41] But tragic and comic hope for reform, as well as tragedy's possibility of catharsis, are missing. The comedy of the grotesque is, according to Ionesco, "more conducive to despair than the tragic. The comic offers no way out."[42] Accordingly, the contemporary novelist of the absurd seeks no reform of a world probably beyond remedy and certainly beyond comprehension. He is not concerned, as Scholes phrases it, "with what to do about life but with how to *take* it."[43] The absurdity of the human condition, if faced squarely, can be viewed as a cosmic joke. Thus, while the novelist of the absurd emphasizes the blackness of modern existence, the response he seeks is neither stoic resignation nor Camusian scorn, but laughter. In this aim he is at one with French dramatists of the absurd, who believe that "the dignity of man lies in his ability to face reality in all its senselessness; to accept it freely, without fear, without illusions—and to laugh at it."[44]

Before concluding this discussion of the aesthetics of absurdity, a word needs to be said about the quality of the absurd vision shared by these novelists. Paul Hurley has maintained that the basic difference between French and American dramatists of the absurd is the incapability of the latter to commit themselves totally to absurdity. While they may believe that society is absurd, American dramatists like Kopit and Albee cannot, it seems, "surrender themselves to a belief that *life* is absurd."[45] Although they give lip-service to absurdity, they inevitably relent in the name of human and social progress. To a degree, what Professor Hurley says of the American dramatists of the absurd holds true for American novelists of the absurd. Their "No! In thunder," while invariably evident in the form of their novels, is often mitigated by a seemingly irresistible affirmation which is sometimes stated flatly by the novelist.

This affirmation should not be confused with the kind of affirmation found in works of existentialism. Contemporary novelists of the absurd begin with the same basic premise as the existentialists—the world is absurd. But they are post-existential in their view of man, generally lacking the existentialist's faith in the human character. From Nietzsche to Camus, existentialists have agreed that, since no God exists to rely on, man must rely upon himself. Nietzsche's faith in the individual human being reached such Romantic proportions that he could envision a Superman. Even Sisyphus, who had his perpetual rock to roll up that mountain, could surmount his absurd circumstances, deriving meaning from his struggle. "One must imagine Sisyphus happy," Camus concludes his famous tract. And Sartre insists that existentialism is a humanism. To the contemporary novelists of the absurd, on the other hand, man is far too puny and helpless for self-reliance.[46]

But a temporary analgesic for existential pain does exist. Love, contemporary absurdist novelists say with Matthew Arnold, while it cannot eradicate the slings and arrows of an outrageously ravaged universe, offers some consolation to those who suffer them. The essence of existence is unquestionably *nada*, but some solace is discoverable in the clean well-lighted places of the human heart. In this respect, these novelists appear unwilling or unable to remain completely true to the vision that life is meaningless. Or at least they do not insist that despair represents the only possible human response to life's absurdity.

The novelist should have the right to his own vision, and

the critic's task—or so it seems to me—should not be to question the validity of that vision but to determine whether or not its presentation is artistically successful. When the novel's affirmative vision clashes with its negative, or absurd, vision, the result is not aesthetically pleasing. The writer tries to hold two contradictory views simultaneously: the world, he seems to say, is both meaningful and meaningless. Because his vision of absurdity is so intense, we find ourselves asking the same question asked by Philip Roth:

> If the world is as crooked and as unreal as . . . it is becoming, day by day; if one feels less and less power in the face of this unreality, day by day; if the inevitable end is destruction, if not of all life, then of much that is valuable and civilized in life— then why in God's name is the writer pleased?[47]

In other words, the writer's affirmative vision strikes us as insincere or at least as contradictory; it seems imposed upon the narrative, forced into the novel's fabric.

At their best, however, these novelists are able to have it both ways. In these instances, the novelist refrains from overt moralization or preachment, allowing the form of his novel to act as his surrogate. The incidents themselves, plus the ways in which the novelist manages his language and other artifices of style, allow the twin themes, absurdity and the need for human love, to grow organically from the novel. When this happens, there is no contradiction, and the novel's affirmation is not obtrusive. In cases like this, these novelists succeed in blending both nihilism and the belief that love can be efficacious into an organic whole which does not jar our aesthetic sensibilities. While their belief that certain human relationships can achieve a small degree of meaning alloys an otherwise absurdist vision, it need not, as evidenced by the best of these novels, mar the artistic achievement of the contemporary American novelists of the absurd. In the following pages I hope to demonstrate the ways in which an absurdist vision forms the central element in the novels of Heller, Vonnegut, Pynchon, and Barth; and how these writers have sometimes failed, but more often succeeded, in presenting that vision.

II

Catch - 22:
A Radical Protest against Absurdity

IN 1961 ex-bomber pilot Joseph Heller dropped his first
novel into the midst of the literary world, scattering
confusion and wounding the sensibilities of many early reviewers. Much of the critical disfavor resulted from a
seeming lack of plan in *Catch-22*. *Time*, for example, complained that Heller's talent, though often impressive, lacked
discipline, "sometimes luring him into bogs of boring repetition."[1] Richard Stern also found the novel "repetitive and
monotonous." In fact, so disturbed was Stern at the apparent lack of "craft and sensibility" in *Catch-22* that he even
refused to call it a novel.[2] Going Stern one better, *The
New Yorker's* Whitney Balliett insisted that *Catch-22* "is
not really a book. It doesn't even seem to have been written; instead it gives the impression of having been shouted
onto paper."[3] Even early admirers expressed confusion at
the novel's apparent formlessness. Robert Brustein, for
example, though describing the novel as "one of the most
bitterly funny works in the language," admitted that it was
"as formless as any picaresque epic."[4] Similarly, Orville
Prescott tempered his admiration by charging that *Catch-22*
is "not . . . a good novel by conventional standards."[5]

Unwittingly perhaps, Prescott's statement comes close to
explaining much of the early criticism against Heller's
novel. Few reviewers in the fall and winter of 1961 recognized what since has come to be generally accepted—that
although *Catch-22* abandons conventional novelistic techniques, it lacks neither craft nor form. Both prose and

structure are carefully controlled, not only to reinforce the novel's theme of absurdity but to create their own dimension of absurdity as well. By treating his absurdist theme with absurdist techniques, Heller introduced a new pattern of literary expression to the American sixties.

Its technical innovations notwithstanding, Heller's novel does operate within an established literary tradition. *Catch-22* is finally a radical protest novel.[6] Like *The Grapes of Wrath* and *An American Tragedy*, its protest is directed from the left toward the prevailing centers of power in America. But whereas Steinbeck and Dreiser aimed their polemics at the trust and the tycoon, Heller's target shifted. As C. Wright Mills points out, the new images of power in modern mass society are the interlocking bureaucracies of industry, the military, and the political administration.[7] Heller apparently feels that the power shift must be countered with new patterns of protest.

Radical novelists of the past, equipped with what Brian Way calls "positivist rationalist assumptions," believed that if they "showed how a railroad was really operated, or what it was like to live and work in a fruit-picking camp, the reader, sharing in the common stock of human reason, would react with the indignation the writer desired."[8] Heller, on the other hand, rejects this rationalist faith. Because he views the objects of his attack as "images of non-reason," Heller has turned from naturalism to "the literature of non-reason . . . for the appropriate means of exploration and criticism."[9]

Since Heller protests against rather than simply presenting absurdity, he differs from other absurdist novelists of the sixties. To be sure, writers such as Barth, Vonnegut, and Pynchon often focus upon the absurdities inherent in modern mass society. Yet they generally view these absurdities as manifestations of a larger absurdity, one that is all-pervasive, cosmic. In this respect these novelists cannot properly be called radical protest novelists because they do not feel society can be reformed. Barth speaks for all of them when he says, "My argument is with the facts of life, not the conditions of it."[10]

Heller, on the other hand, refuses to accept absurdity as an ontological fact. Rather, he views it as a by-product of the bureaucracies in control of modern mass society. In *Catch-22* the military serves as a metaphor for bureaucratic power in general. As the novel develops, this power spreads until it seems to touch all aspects of human life. Yossarian, the novel's protagonist, is temporarily safe from the destructive influence of the military, for example, when he is on leave in Rome or in the hospital. Eventually, however, these retreats are either destroyed or transformed by the cancer-like spread of bureaucratic power. M.P.'s drive the prostitutes from the Rome brothel, depriving Yossarian of the temporary solace of sex. Indeed, the only prostitute remaining, Nately's whore, becomes in her attempts upon Yossarian's life an ironic embodiment of the ubiquitous and unreasoned death heretofore associated with the military. Rome, itself, elsewhere in the novel a symbol of sanity and the good life, is here transformed into a distorted nightmare of violence and unreason.

Similarly, the hospital, "where they couldn't dominate Death ... but they certainly made her behave,"[11] is viewed by Yossarian through most of the novel as a place of relative sanity and health. Late in the novel, however, the return of "the soldier in white" transforms the hospital into a chamber of horrors and confusion. The reappearance of "the soldier in white," who has already been declared dead by Nurse Cramer, seems proof of the Army's power to dole out death arbitrarily, then change its mind. As James M. Mellard suggests, Yossarian

> ... cannot be certain that [the soldier in white's] death is *not* the responsibility of some official act, like Nurse Cramer's, some *official* "decision to terminate," a "disappearance" like Dunbar's and Major Major's and Major —— de Coverly's, or a bureaucratic "death" like that of Doc Daneeka, who is physically alive but technically dead because he was supposed to be on a plane that crashed killing all the crew.[12]

These insidious bureaucratic "deaths" are a matter of policy, not of the victim's loss of health, and are more to be feared than death by violence.

Such bureaucratic decisions to "terminate with extreme prejudice" reveal another major concern of *Catch-22*. Like most radical protest novelists, Heller resents the effect the power structure has upon individual lives. The bureaucracy influences the personality of almost every character in *Catch-22*. On the one hand, characters like Colonel Cathcart, the commanding officer on Pianosa, and young Milo Minderbinder, mess officer turned entrepreneur, have learned the "rules" of their bureaucratic system and, according to the standards of that system, have become successful. Less fortunate are figures like A. T. Tappman, group chaplain, and Major Major, squadron officer at Pianosa. Heller depicts Tappman as an "almost good-looking [man], with a pleasant, sensitive" face. Earnest, gentle, and sincere, Tappman possesses a mind "open on every subject." Such traits, however, bear little relevance to a bureaucratic society, which rewards only "aggressive men of action like Col. Cathcart." Consequently, "in a world in which success was the only virtue," the potentially useful chaplain "had resigned himself to failure" (262). Like Tappman, Major Major falls victim to a society he cannot understand.

> He was polite to his elders, who disliked him. Whatever his elders told him to do, he did. ... He was told to honor his father and his mother, and he honored his father and his mother. He was told that he should not kill, and he did not kill, until he got into the Army. Then he was told to kill, and he killed. He turned the other cheek on every occasion and always did unto others exactly as he would have had others do unto him. ... He never once took the name of the Lord his God in vain, committed adultery or coveted his neighbor's ass. In fact, he loved his neighbor and never even bore false witness • against him. Major Major's elders disliked him because he was such a flagrant nonconformist. (84)

The dichotomy between actions and values forms part of the "rules" of a bureaucratic society. Neither Tappman nor Major Major can understand these hypocritical rules. Thus, they resign themselves to confusion and failure.

A third kind of character in the novel refuses to abide

by the rules of the bureaucratic system or to fall victim to that system. Dr. Stubbs openly opposes the system. When he disobeys orders by grounding fliers for medical reasons, the military immediately transfers him to the Pacific. Unlike Stubbs, Orr, Yossarian's pixie-like roommate, realizes how futile attempts to fight the system would be. Rather than fight the system, then, Orr escapes it. He cultivates "a look of stupid innocence that nobody would ever suspect of any cleverness" (439) and actually practices "getting shot down" on most of his missions. On one mission, Orr allows himself to be shot down, then rows in a tiny yellow life raft all the way to neutral Sweden. Such "a miracle of human perseverance" convinces Yossarian that escape is possible and leads to his own desertion near the novel's end. Orr's escape also reveals Heller's faith in the abilities of the individual human being, a faith shared by most radical protest novelists.

Yossarian chooses flight shortly after Milo's Enterprises, representative in the novel of the industrial bureaucracy, merges with the military to form a seemingly infrangible military-industrial complex, international in scope. Little hope remains that Yossarian will be able to find even temporary respite from bureaucratic influence. His decision to escape must be seen as an escape not only from the industrial-military bureaucracy but from the absurdity it embodies. The belief that Yossarian can escape absurdity even if he cannot obviate it sharply distinguishes Heller's vision from the vision of other absurdist novelists of the sixties, who see absurdity as an irremediable and inescapable fact of the human condition. As Frederick Karl indicates, Heller's protest is that of "the idealist who can never accept that moral values have become insignificant or meaningless in human conduct."[13] Despite the absurdist form of *Catch-22*, its optimistic ending suggests that the novel not only protests absurdity but rejects it as ultimate reality.

Its radical optimism notwithstanding, *Catch-22* may be seen as the first American novel of the absurd to appear in the sixties. Its technical innovations distinguish it from the novels that precede it and link it with the absurdist novels which follow it. It is largely through technique, in fact, that Heller levels his protest at modern bureaucratic power. These techniques fall into three main categories. Burlesque is perhaps the favorite weapon used by Heller in his attack on the bureaucracies. Unlike other absurdist novelists of the sixties, however, Heller burlesques only the object and never the vehicle of his protest. That is, his use of burlesque is non-reflexive, an example of Heller's faith in the power of literature to bring about change. A second means by which Heller conveys the sense of the absurd is his use of language. The prose Heller uses to describe certain absurd incidents often contributes to the lunacy of those incidents. Finally, the structure of *Catch-22*, so often misunderstood, reflects in its total rejection of an orderly time sequence the disjointed world Heller is examining.

As portrayed by Heller, the military bureaucracy is little more than the absurd institutionalized. Its hierarchical structure and its wanton use of "military logic" are mere pretenses of order and reason, masks to hide its essential absurdity. By burlesquing military activities, Heller strikes through the mask, exposing the unreason which lurks behind.

Heller portrays the carefully ordered military hierarcy as nothing more than structured chaos. Chief Halfoat, for instance, is an illiterate intelligence officer. Corporal Whitcomb, an atheist, is assistant to the chaplain. Aarfy is a navigator without a sense of direction. The most absurd assignment of all involves Major Major. Promoted to major by a faulty IBM machine, Major Major is sent to cadet school where he outranks Lieutenant Scheisskopf, his commanding officer. Both men wind up calling each other "Sir." Rather than admit its error, the Air Force continues to promote the hapless major until he finally becomes squadron officer at Pianosa. Such absurdities matter little so long as the appearance of order is maintained.

This appearance of order depends largely upon a kind of perverse logic. The main target of Heller's burlesque is this specious "military logic." One example occurs during the question and answer period at the bi-weekly "educational sessions" on Pianosa. Yossarian, paraphrasing Villon's famous question, asks, "Where are the Snowdens of yesteryear," Snowden being the young gunner killed over Avignon in a plane piloted by Yossarian. The question disturbs Group Headquarters, "for there was no telling what people might find out once they felt free to ask whatever questions they wanted to" (35). Displaying a brilliant aptitude for military logic, Colonel Korn rules that thereafter only people who never ask questions can ask questions at the sessions. Of course the sessions soon dissolve, since "it was neither possible nor necessary to educate people who never questioned anything" (35).

Another example occurs when Yossarian flies twice over a bridge at Ferrara, destroying the bridge the second time but getting Kraft killed in the process. Colonel Cathcart faces a dilemma. "I don't give a damn about the man or the airplane," he explains to Yossarian. "It's just that it looks so lousy on the report. How am I going to cover up something like this in the report?" (136) Colonel Korn, master of military logic, again provides the solution. "Why don't we give him a medal?" he proposes. "You know, that might be the answer—to act boastfully about something we ought to be ashamed of. That's a trick that never seems to fail." Not only is Yossarian decorated for Ferrara, but he is also promoted to captain.

Indeed, what happens on the field of battle matters little, so long as the appearance of order is maintained within the Bomber Group's administrative network. When Yossarian moves the bomb line on the operations map to a position north of Bologna, the city under siege at that point, the entire Mediterranean theater of war is convinced that the city has fallen. The official records, not the facts, matter. In fact, records and communications are so important to the apparent order of the bureaucracy that the most powerful man in the entire Bomber Group is ex-PFC Wintergreen, who is in charge of communications.

Should reality and the official records clash, reality must yield. When McWatt, distraught over killing Kid Sampson, crashes his plane into the side of a mountain, Doc Daneeka, whose name had appeared on the official flight list, is also declared dead. Though obviously alive, Doc is treated from that moment on as if he doesn't exist. The records are absolute. Mudd, the "dead man in Yossarian's tent," receives similar treatment. Because he had reported to the wrong tent upon his arrival at Pianosa, Mudd does not receive official credit for ever having reported to the squadron at all. He is killed two hours later over Orvieto, but his name cannot be removed from the official roster since it was never officially added. Just as Doc Daneeka, still very much alive, is dead according to bureaucratic logic, so Mudd, quite dead, is denied death. Moreover, Mudd's be-belongings cannot be removed from Yossarian's tent despite Yossarian's constant complaints, since if Mudd never existed his gear cannot exist.

The major device in the novel by which the military makes the irrational appear rational is "catch-22." Catch-22 is a "rule" that possesses a different clause for every occasion requiring its use. When Doc Daneeka refuses Yossarian's request to be grounded because of insanity, for example, the following explanation is offered:

> There was only one catch and that was Catch-22, which specified that a concern for one's own safety in the face of dangers that were real and immediate was the process of a rational mind. Orr was crazy and could be grounded. All he had to do was ask; and as soon as he did, he would no longer be crazy and would have to fly more missions. Orr would be crazy to fly more missions and sane if he didn't, but if he was sane he had to fly them. If he flew them he was crazy and didn't have to; but if he didn't want to he was sane and had to. Yossarian was moved very deeply by the absolute simplicity of this clause of Catch-22. . . . (46)

Again, when Yossarian discovers that Colonel Cathcart's constant raising of the required number of missions conflicts with the number required by Air Force Headquarters, he is told that he must obey Cathcart's orders nonetheless.

> "Catch-22," Doc Daneeka answered patiently, . . . "says you've always got to do what your commanding officer tells you to."

"But Twenty-seventh Air Force says I can go home with forty missions."

"But they don't say you have to go home. And regulations do say you have to obey every order. That's the catch. Even if the colonel were disobeying a Twenty-seventh Air Force order by making you fly more missions, you'd still have to fly them, or you'd be guilty of disobeying an order of his. And then Twenty-seventh Air Force Headquarters would really jump on you." (58)

Finally, when the MP's destroy the Rome brothel, chasing the whores into the night, their right to do so is guaranteed by catch-22. In fact, as the MP's tell the old madam, catch-22 allows the military to do whatever it is strong enough to do, and it is strong enough to do just about anything. Yet catch-22 is never precisely defined, an indefiniteness—as Yossarian perceives—that assures its invulnerability. "Catch-22 did not exist, he was positive of that, but it made no difference. What did matter was that everyone thought it existed, and that was much worse, for there was no object or text to ridicule or refute, to accuse, criticize, attack, amend, hate, revile, spit at, rip to shreds, trample upon or burn" (400). As Brian Way suggests, catch-22 "is the infinite capacity of the absurd to mask itself in reason."[14]

Such absurdity would not be as frightening were it confined to the military. As the novel progresses, however, absurdity spreads, eventually encompassing the entire Western world, with only places like Sweden, both "neutral" and socialistic, remaining immune. In the wake of absurdity, traditional values are swept under. Profit, "efficiency," even good public relations, take precedence over humane considerations. The growth of Milo's Enterprises, for example, involves not only the adoption of certain military tactics, such as bomb raids, but the use of the same pseudo-logic to explain those tactics that characterizes catch-22. To boost the financial stability of M&M Enterprises, Milo contracts with the Germans to bomb his own base. Milo faces disgrace for his collaboration with the enemy:

Not one voice was raised in his defense. Decent people everywhere were affronted, and Milo was all washed up until he opened his books to the public and disclosed the tremendous profit he had made. He could reimburse the government for all the people and property he had destroyed and still have enough money left over to continue buying Egyptian cotton. Everybody, of course, owned a share. And the sweetest part of the whole deal was that there really was no need to reimburse the government at all [since] the government is the people.... (255)

Needless to say, Milo is exonerated completely.

The entire capitalistic world shares Milo's utilitarian business ethic. Doc Daneeka's avaricious medical practice, for example, is the rule not the exception. In fact, Dr. Stubbs jeopardizes the "good name" of the medical profession "by standing up for principles" (343). Stubbs disobeys orders by grounding certain fliers for medical reasons. Similarly, Sergeant Whitcomb, displaying his customary bureaucratic zeal, rejoices at the deaths of twelve fliers because that "meant twelve more form letters of condolence ... could be mailed in one bunch to the next of kin over Colonel Cathcart's signature, giving Sergeant Whitcomb hope of getting an article on Colonel Cathcart into *The Saturday Evening Post* in time for Easter" (370-71).

Not only do profit motives supersede humane motives in a world devoted to bureaucratic efficiency, but mediocrity often supersedes ability. Colonel Cargill's success as a marketing executive depends upon his ineptitude. Able to "run the most prosperous enterprise into the ground," Cargill is much in demand by firms eager to establish losses for tax purposes. Similarly, Major Major's father specializes in not growing alfalfa. "The government paid him well for every bushel of alfalfa he did not grow. The more alfalfa he did not grow, the more money the government gave him, and he spent every penny he didn't earn on new land to increase the amount of alfalfa he did not produce. ... He invested in land wisely and soon was not growing more alfalfa than any other man in the county" (82). Success and failure are not such strange bedfellows in a country dominated by bureaucratic logic.

Indeed, in Yossarian's topsy-turvy world the bizarre becomes the usual. Dunbar cultivates boredom so that time, a precious commodity in a war period, will pass more slowly. Yossarian abstains from eating fruit because fruit is good for his bad liver and a bad liver, in time of war, is an asset. The sensitive Major Major, thoroughly disliked by the enlisted men because of his rank, allows visitors in his office only when he is out. Mess sergeant Snark mashes soap into the sweet potatoes and the men clamor for more, not because they "have the taste of Philistines," as Snark suspects, but because a sick squadron means canceled missions. And so on. As he burlesques the absurd conditions of an insane world, Heller never loses sight of his target: the bureaucracies he feels cause these conditions. Underlying his considerable humor is a seriousness bordering upon outrage.

A second method by which Heller suggests absurdity is his use of language. A recurring device of this nature is the tautological dialogue, circular conversations filled with much sound but little sense. The Action Board's examination of Clevinger, the idealistic and impractical intellectual, contains a good example of this kind of dialogue. At one point in the "trial," which is an effective parody of a McCarthy hearing gone mad (or perhaps madder), Clevinger is asked the following question:

"... Just what the hell did you mean, you bastard, when you said we couldn't punish you?"
... "I didn't say you couldn't punish me, sir."
"When?" asked the colonel.
"When what, sir?"
"Now you're asking me questions...."
"I'm sorry, sir. I'm afraid I don't understand your question."
"When didn't you say we couldn't punish you? Don't you understand my question?"
"No, sir. I don't understand."
"You've just told us that. Now suppose you answer my question."
"But how can I answer it?"
"That's another question you're asking me."

"I'm sorry sir. But I don't know how to answer it. I never said you couldn't punish me."

"Now you're telling us when you did say it. I'm asking you to tell us when you didn't say it."

Clevinger took a deep breath. "I always didn't say you couldn't punish me, sir."

"That's much better, Mr. Clevinger, even though it is a barefaced lie. . . ." (76)

Clevinger's mind reels with the dialogue which circles sense but never lights on it. Such concentricity reflects the specious logic of the Action Board whose members feel it their patriotic duty to find Clevinger guilty. After all, they reason, were he innocent he would not have been charged in the first place.

In the name of order, the Action Board purveys its nonsense. Not only is justice lost in the transaction, but any actual communication is impossible. The breakdown of communication between men in *Catch-22*, as Sanford Pinkser suggests, shows symptomatically the breakdown of an orderly universe.[15] The tautological dialogue reflects this breakdown of order. At times, a conversation rambles for pages in the novel, only to end up where it began, with no information having been exchanged. Notice, for example, this circular conversation between Yossarian and Milo.

" . . . You see, I don't really have a liver condition. I've just got the symptoms. I have a Garnett-Fleischaker syndrome."

"I see," said Milo. "And what is a Garnett-Fleischaker syndrome?"

"A liver condition."

"I see," said Milo, . . . "In that case . . . I suppose you do have to be very careful about what you eat, don't you?"

"Very careful, indeed," Yossarian told him. "A good Garnett-Fleischaker syndrome isn't easy to come by, and I don't want to ruin mine. That's why I never eat any fruit."

"Now I do see," said Milo. "Fruit is bad for your liver?"

"No, fruit is good for my liver. That's why I never eat any." (60-61)

Milo's confused response is, "Yes, now I see. But I still don't . . . understand" (60), a comment that could well follow each of the tautological conversations in the novel. Through these incomprehensible dialogues, Heller reflects the breakdown of language and logic in the absurd world of *Catch-22.*

A second linguistic device by which Heller reflects absurdity is the comic reversal. This device can best be explained through an example. In describing the Texan who shares the hospital ward with Yossarian, Heller writes: "The Texan turned out to be good-natured, generous and likable." Such a description sets up a certain expectation on the part of the reader, namely, that the Texan, if likable, will indeed be liked by Yossarian and the other patients in the ward. In the very next sentence, however, Heller dashes this expectation. "In three days," he writes, "no one could stand him" (9). A similar passage concerns Nurse Cramer's freckles. "Nurse Cramer had a cute nose and a radiant, blooming complexion dotted with fetching sprays of adorable freckles that Yossarian detested" (167). Such constructions, with their unexpected reversals, suggest a world in which the unexpected ·is the usual. By demanding an inversion of the reader's normal response, they suggest a world in which traditional responses and values have also been inverted, a condition that we have seen depicted in other ways in the novel.

Heller employs several variations upon the comic reversal. One, the "wrenched cliché," results from changing a key word in an otherwise hackneyed expression. For example, Yossarian characterizes Dunbar as "a true prince. One of the finest, *least* dedicated men in the whole world" (14, italics added). Similarly, Doc Daneeka is described as "Yossarian's friend," one who "would do just about *nothing* in his power to help him" (28, italics added). The substitution of an unexpected word for the expected one reflects the unpredictability of a world rendered absurd by bureaucracy.

A second variation on the reversal involves juxtaposed incongruities. This device works most effectively in Heller's description of Colonel Cathcart. A true organization man, Cathcart—who wants to be general—strives eagerly to conform to the military ideal. But the military is absurd and its rules and taboos (like the elusive catch-22) are constantly shifting. As a result, Cathcart, though confident of his progress up the road of success, fears constantly that he will somehow violate a rule of the road. Through a prose style containing juxtaposed words, phrases, and clauses that express contradictory ideas, Heller conveys the conflicting moods of Colonel Cathcart. For example, Cathcart is described as both "dashing and dejected, poised and cha-grinned. He was complacent and insecure, daring in the administrative stratagems he employed to bring himself to the attention of his superiors and craven in his concern that his schemes might all backfire" (185). Furthermore, Cathcart is "tense, irritable, bitter and smug. . . . He believed all the news he heard and had faith in none. . . . He was someone in the know who was always striving pathetically to find out what was going on" (186). Such juxtaposed incongruities hilariously convey the acute insecurity of the social conformist who desperately seeks accommodation with the protean forms of an absurd society.

Heller uses language to reinforce his theme of absurdity in yet a third way. He describes a scene in serious, often inflated prose, usually extending the description over at least a paragraph; but suddenly, the seriousness—or mock-seriousness, as is often the case—gives way to the trivial or ludicrous, producing an anti-climactic effect. A good example of Heller's use of anti-climax occurs during the forest confrontation of the Chaplain and Captain Flume, the "wild Hermit of the woods."

> The captain nodded, and the chaplain gazed at his porous, gray pallor of fatigue and malnutrition with a mixture of pity and esteem. The man's body was a bony shell inside rumpled clothing that hung on him like a disorderly collection of sacks. Wisps of dried grass were glued all over him; he needed a haircut badly. There were great, dark circles under his eyes. The chaplain was moved almost to tears by the harassed, bedraggled picture the captain presented, and he filled with deference and compassion at the thought of the many severe rigors the poor man had to endure daily. In a voice hushed with humility, he said, "Who does your laundry?" (272-73)

Once again, Heller's prose emphasizes the lack of predictability in a world gone mad. Predictability depends on logical cause-and-effect relationships. In an absurd universe, however, such relationships are non-existent. Instead, effects are commonly bizarre, illogical, unpredictable, and totally independent of what has gone before.

As I indicated at the beginning of this chapter, many early reviewers felt *Catch-22* lacked any organizing principle. Instead, they found the novel repetitious and formless. Not until 1967 did an article attempting to examine the structure of *Catch-22* appear. Jan Solomon argued that *Catch-22* has not one but two orderly time-sequences. The part of the novel focusing on Yossarian is marked by psychological time, moving "forward and back from a pivotal point in time," that point at which Yossarian flees to the hospital after the missions are raised to forty-five. The second time-sequence, focusing on Milo, moves chronologically, "directly forward," from one of Milo's successes to the next. "Independently," Solomon maintains, "each chronology is valid and logical; together, the two time-sequences are impossible." The structural absurdity resulting from the crossing of these "mutually contradictory chronologies" enforces "the absurdity of character and event in the novel."[16]

In 1968 three more articles appeared, each seconding Solomon's contention that *Catch-22* is carefully structured. Both James McDonald and James Mellard comment on Heller's use of *déjà vu* as a structural principle. For McDonald, the repetitions in *Catch-22* exemplify how "the past operates in the present by forming the individual's apprehensions of the present, coloring and outlining each significant moment." The novel's overall structure, McDonald continues, can be described "as an interplay between present narrative and the cumulative repetition and gradual clarification of past actions."[17] Mellard agrees with McDonald that the events in the novel are ordered by Yossarian's consciousness, but he interprets the reason for the repetitions in the novel differently. To Mellard, these repetitions represent certain "repressed desires, needs, or memories" as they try to penetrate Yossarian's "ego-consciousness." Because these desires and memories conflict with Yossarian's military obligations, he repeatedly "censors" them. Thus Yossarian's realization of them takes a long time. The novel's development is determined by "Yossarian's painful recognition of his own mortality and personal involvement, [and] his acceptance of individual guilt and a need for a new set of values."[18]

While not exclusively concerned with structure, the third of these articles appearing in 1968 devotes several pages to that important problem. Unlike Solomon, Brian Way maintains that "it is impossible to establish an orderly time-sequence for the novel."[19] Unlike McDonald and Mellard, Way does not believe the events of the novel are filtered through Yossarian's consciousness. In fact, he insists that the "progression and development of *Catch-22*" are not to be seen "in a mechanical advance of incident and plot" at all. Rather, the novel develops through a "qualitative change in the nature of its comedy," which moves "effortlessly" from the farce of the novel's early pages to eventual protest and horror.[20]

Way's comments about the structure of *Catch-22* are more nearly correct. Solomon's argument to the contrary, there is no orderly time-sequence in *Catch-22*. Heller deliberately inserts references to relative time throughout the novel, but any attempt to link these references into logical time sequence proves futile. A number of examples can be cited to prove this contention, but one should suffice. We know that Snowden is killed over Avignon about a week before a nude Yossarian is decorated for bombing the bridge at Ferrara (215). We also know that this decoration occurs before the Great Big Siege of Bologna, since during the second week of that siege Colonel Cathcart reminds Colonel Korn that Yossarian is "the man you made me give a medal to after Ferrara" (123). Even Solomon agrees to this apparently clearly stated time-sequence.[21] Immediately after Bologna, Yossarian secures a rest leave and rushes to Rome "where he found Luciana and her invisible scar that same night" (151). He sleeps with Luciana, bids her "addio," tears up the address she gives him, then has second thoughts and begins a frantic search for her. To this point, it is clear that each of these events has occurred after Avignon and the death of Snowden. Yet the morning after his fruitless search for Luciana, a distraught Yossarian runs to Snowden's apartment for the always willing maid in lime-colored panties. "*Snowden was still alive then*," writes Heller, confounding an otherwise logical time-sequence (162, italics added). Indeed, the only apparent reason Heller has for mentioning Snowden at this particular point in the narrative is to confuse the chronology of events.

In other words, Heller purposely entangles chronology as part of his absurdist method. His hints of a logical time order where none exists reflect the pretense of logic and order with which the bureaucracies mask their absurdity. Even these hints are often vague and ambiguous, as in the following example.

> Yossarian ... knew exactly who Mudd was. Mudd was the unknown soldier who ... was really unknown, even though his belongings still lay in a tumble on the cot in Yossarian's tent almost exactly as he had left them *three months earlier* the day he never arrived—all contaminated with death less than two hours later, in the same way that all was contaminated with death *the very next week* during the Great Big Siege of Bologna when the moldy odor of mortality hung wet in the air.... (107)

Although the passages I have italicized seem to contain clear references to relative time, a closer investigation proves the information worthless. We are told that Mudd left his belongings on Yossarian's cot "three months earlier." Earlier than when? When is present-time in the passage? And does Bologna occur "the very next week" after Mudd's death, or after present-time in the passage, whenever that is? These questions are finally unanswerable. Apparently clear references to an orderly time sequence are nothing more than useless facts. By denying a temporal order, Heller strengthens his portrait of a disordered universe. As Way points out, "For Heller, the war is an unchanging condition of absurdity and terror, and it would be a falsification to suggest that there could be any orderly development of this situation, in time, towards a resolution."[22]

This lack of a coherent time-sequence in *Catch-22* suggests the absence of conventional stream-of-consciousness techniques, despite contentions to the contrary by McDonald and Mellard. Both critics believe the events in the novel are ordered by Yossarian's consciousness. To be sure, certain events do seem to be presented from Yossarian's point of view. But events are presented from the points of view of Tappman, Major Major, Dunbar and Colonel Cathcart, also. One might argue that a variety of streams of consciousness flow through the novel, but such a contention creates more problems than it solves.

An earlier draft of *Catch-22* did contain intermittent streams of consciousness, but Heller thoroughly revised that draft in writing the final version of his novel.[23] In this final version, Heller abandoned most novelistic conventions of the past altogether. Consequently, any attempt to read *Catch-22* as a conventional stream-of-consciousness novel is to force it into what Heller obviously considers an outworn form. Indeed, more evidence in the novel argues against its interpretation as a stream-of-consciousness novel than otherwise. Stream-of-consciousness novels involute time; they don't destroy it. They deny the relevance of chronological order, not the existence of it. Even events in such a highly involuted novel as *The Sound and the Fury* can be chronologically arranged, as Edmund Volpe has demonstrated.[24] Similar attempts to order the events in *Catch-22*, however, seemed doomed to failure.

In the final analysis, all that is traditional about *Catch-22* is its protest. Its technical innovations, on the other hand, represent a radical departure from the fictional formulas of the past. Heller's use of burlesque, the way his language reinforces the absurdity it describes, and a structure that denies logical order all constitute breakthroughs that are vitally new to the American novel. Thus *Catch-22* is an important book. With its publication in 1961, the Decade of the Absurd had begun.

III

Illusion and Absurdity:
The Novels of Kurt Vonnegut, Jr.

CRITICS have variously categorized Kurt Vonnegut, Jr. He has been called a writer of science fiction, a black humorist, and a satirist.[1] Part of this confusion derives from the variety of types of novels Vonnegut has written. His first two novels, although clearly belonging to the science fiction genre, differ markedly. *Player Piano* (1952) has been called "the best of all the recent anti-utopias."[2] *The Sirens of Titan* (1959), on the other hand, though exhibiting many features characteristic of science fiction, is really an extended comic metaphor for a purposeless universe. *Mother Night* (1961), Vonnegut's third novel, makes a powerful little statement against the kinds of social attitudes responsible for war and its atrocities. In Vonnegut's three most recent novels, however, a discernible pattern begins to emerge. *Cat's Cradle* (1963), *God Bless You, Mr. Rosewater, or Pearls Before Swine* (1965), and *Slaughterhouse-Five, or The Children's Crusade* (1969) all display that treatment of absurdist themes with absurdist techniques characteristic of the other novels treated in this study, the contemporary novels of the absurd.

Of the absurdist novelists considered in this study, Vonnegut enjoys the largest general readership. This popularity evolved slowly, however, a fact reflected in Vonnegut's publishing history. His first four books—the three novels already mentioned and *Canary in a Cat House* (1961), a collection of short stories no longer in print—appeared initially in paperback.[3] In 1961, Houghton Mifflin reissued *The Sirens of Titan* in hardbound, the first book of Vonnegut's to appear in a hard-cover edition. Holt, Rinehart, and Winston published *Cat's Cradle* in 1963, the first of Vonnegut's novels to appear originally in hardbound. The same publishing house issued *God Bless You, Mr. Rosewater* in 1964 and republished *Player Piano* in hardbound in 1966. While teaching at the University of Iowa's Writer's Workshop, Vonnegut met Seymour Lawrence who signed him to a three-book contract for the Delacorte Press. Vonnegut's two latest books, *Welcome to the Monkey House* (1968), a collection of short stories, and *Slaughterhouse-Five*, partially fulfill that contract. So in their various editions, Vonnegut's eight books have gone through seven different publishers. With Delacorte, however, Vonnegut seems to have found a home. *Slaughterhouse-Five* was something of a literary "event," receiving a front-page review in the prestigious *The New York Times Book Review* and rising quickly to the *Times* best-seller list. Moreover, C. D. B. Bryan has recently detected the beginnings of a Vonnegut cult among university students.[4] Vonnegut's popular success therefore seems assured.

Vonnegut's impression upon the academic critics, however, has been less than sensational. In fact, as late as 1969 only two studies devoted exclusively to Vonnegut's works had appeared, and one of these was in Italian.[5] Several possible reasons for this critical snub exist. The most obvious seems to be that many of Vonnegut's early stories were of the "slick" variety. As Leslie Fiedler points out in a recent essay, an almost religiously adhered-to distinction between *belles-lettres* and popular art, high culture and low, accompanied the advent of new criticism. Most "serious" works of literary art written during the period of early twentieth-century modernism were "essentially self-aware, . . . dedicated to analysis, rationality, anti-romantic dialectic—and, consequently, aimed at respectability, gentility, even academicism."[6] Writers whose books lacked this "self-awareness" were dismissed by the critics as "popular" and summarily ignored. Witness, for example, the fates of Somerset Maugham in England and John O'Hara in America. Vonnegut, too, suffered such critical condescension. "When I was supporting myself as a freelance writer doing stories for the *Saturday Evening Post* and *Colliers*," he complains, "I was *scorned*! I mean, there was a time when to be a slick writer was a disgusting thing to be, as though it were prostitution." Vonnegut wrote the commercial stories for a simple reason: he lacked money to support his family. "The people who did not write for the slicks obviously did not need the money. I would have liked very much to have been that sort of person, but I wasn't. I was the head of a family, supporting the damn thing in what seemed—to me, at least—an honorable way. During most of my freelancing I made what I would have made in charge of the cafeteria at a pretty good junior-high school."[7]

The works of science fiction Vonnegut wrote early in his career may also contribute to the reluctance with which critics have accepted him as a "serious" writer. Leslie Fiedler includes science fiction with the western and pornography as those genres "most associated with exploitation by the mass media,"[8] and Vonnegut himself has said that "people regard science-fiction writers as interchangeable with comic-strip writers."[9] Recently, this attitude toward science fiction has shifted. Studies such as Mark Hillegas' *The Future as Nightmare* have helped lift the genre to a level more worthy of serious consideration by academic critics. Nonetheless, Vonnegut broke away from science-fiction after his first two novels, as he explains, because "I thought it was narrowing my readership."[10]

This obvious concern for a wide readership must also dismay certain critics. For at least a generation, critics have been nurtured on portraits of the "pure" artist, responsible only to his art, doggedly determined to shape a new literary conscience for his race rather than submit to the old. Insofar as his technical innovations are concerned, Vonnegut operates in this tradition. On the other hand, however, he openly courts his reader's approbation. For example, Vonnegut insists that he keeps his novels short—they seldom exceed two hundred pages—because he knows that people in power, the politicians and generals, have little time to read long books. He also claims to slant his novels toward university audiences so he can catch future "Presidents and Senators and generals . . . before they become generals and Senators and Presidents, and . . . *pollute their minds with humanity*. Encourage them to make a better world."[11]   Moreover, though science plays an important role in his novels, Vonnegut never depends upon the more technical aspects of science to make his point, as, say, Pynchon does. This is significant when one remembers that Vonnegut majored in chemistry at Cornell and must be technically versed in some areas of scientific theory.

Considerations such as these seem to support Fiedler's contention that "a closing of the gap between elite and mass culture is precisely the function of the novel now."[12] *New* American novelists, among whom Fiedler includes Vonnegut, write the "pop" novel, both "anti-art" and "anti-serious."[13]   To an extent, novels of the absurd may be considered "anti-art," for reasons discussed in Chapter One. But one misses the point if he considers Vonnegut's novels "anti-serious." From the standpoint of both theme and craft, Vonnegut's novels are quite serious, a point to which we must now turn.

The main concern of Vonnegut's novels is the illusions men live by. These illusions fall into two categories. On the one hand, Vonnegut treats those illusions that make human existence more miserable than it need be. The significance man attaches to such artificial distinctions as race, nationality, even national dogma, forces him to overlook the common humanity that links all men. Like Howard Campbell, Jr., the protagonist of *Mother Night*, Vonnegut cannot "think in terms of boundaries. Those imaginary lines are as unreal . . . as elves and pixies. I can't believe that they mark the end or the beginning of anything of real concern to a human soul."[14]   Campbell, however, sees more clearly than most men. He perceives, for example, that as a former counter-intelligence agent for the United States during

World War II, he had performed his role as Nazi propagandist with unnecessary zeal. For such "crimes against himself," he commits suicide (192).

Most men avoid such guilt, however, through what Vonnegut calls "that simple and widespread boon to modern mankind—schizophrenia" (123). Schizophrenia allows men to rationalize certain of their actions that may be inconsistent with the values they hold. Vonnegut refers to such powers of rationalization in his introduction to *Mother Night.* "If I'd been born in Germany," he writes, "I suppose I would have *been* a Nazi, bopping Jews and gypsies and Poles around, leaving boots sticking out of snowbanks, warming myself with my secretly virtuous insides" (vii). *Secretly virtuous insides* is the key phrase here. Campbell's ability to rationalize his effectiveness as a "[whore] in the interest of espionage" (xi) derived from his awareness that "a very good me, the real me, a me made in heaven, is hidden deep inside" (41). Like Sartre, however, Vonnegut seems convinced that "man is nothing else but what he purposes, . . . he is therefore nothing else but the sum of his actions, nothing else but what his life is."[15] The realization of this fact leads Campbell to suicide. The failure to realize it, on the other hand, accounts for what Campbell calls the crime of our times: serving "evil too openly and good too secretly" (xii).

Vonnegut burlesques the lengths to which men go to rationalize their prejudices in his characterization of the Rev. Dr. Lionel J. D. Jones, DDS, DD. Jones edits a neo-Nazi newspaper called *The White Christian Minuteman.* As both Christian and Nazi, Jones has trouble reconciling himself to the widely held assumption that Jesus was Jewish. Employing his own theory that the jaws and teeth of Negroes and Jews prove "beyond question" the degeneracy of these groups, Jones "solves" his dilemma, publishing his findings in a book entitled *Christ Was Not a Jew.* The book, which Vonnegut wryly observes "combined not only dentistry and theology, but the fine arts as well," contained reproductions of fifty famous paintings of Jesus. "According to Jones, not one painting showed Jewish jaws or teeth" (60).

When faith in such distinctions grows especially fervent, war often results. Vonnegut burlesques this possibility in his characterization of Robert Sterling Wilson, the cartoon-like "Black Fuehrer of Harlem," a Negro imprisoned in 1942 as a Japanese spy. A racist, Wilson insists the "colored" peoples of the world are rapidly developing a hydrogen bomb of their own. Japan deserves the honor of dropping the first bomb and will drop it, of all places, upon China. " 'On other colored people?' " Campbell asks Jones. " 'Who ever told you a Chinaman was a colored man' " is Jones's caustic reply.

Jones's convictions lie beyond rational argument. As Swift has said, it is impossible to reason a man out of a position he was not reasoned into. More disturbing than the irrational quality of prejudice, however, is its ability to masquerade as patriotism, convinced that all the forces of righteousness support its cause. "There are plenty of good reasons for fighting," Campbell tells Bernard B. O'Hare, the lieutenant who first arrested Campbell as a war criminal, "but no good reason ever to hate without reservation, to imagine that God Almighty Himself hates with you, too. Where's evil? It's that large part of every man that wants to hate without limit, that wants to hate with God on its side" (181). For such hatred, men die, convinced they have died not for prejudice but *pro patria*—for one's country, "any country at all," as Horlick Minton, ambassador to San Lorenzo, mutters near the end of *Cat's Cradle*.

Like the illusions caused by nationalism and racial prejudice, what might be called the Great-American-Success-Illusion also fosters invidious distinctions. As portrayed by Vonnegut, this illusion impels the judgment of others on the basis of material wealth and "use" to society. A man's worth depends upon what he has, not upon what he is. Consequently, the people most in need of sympathy and aid—the ignorant, the poor, the ill-educated—are the ones most often denied these commodities. As David L. Bazelon has indicated:

... most problems concerning the responsibility of society finally come down to a question of the *allocation of resources* —material and emotional; what we give and what we fail to give; finally understanding and money. One might even say, love and money.[16]

Eliot Rosewater, heir to the multi-million dollar Rosewater Foundation, freely donates his love and money to the near-indigent citizens of Rosewater, Indiana, in *God Bless You, Mr. Rosewater, or Pearls Before Swine.* To an extent, money proves easy to give. The citizens of Rosewater represent America's disinherited, the victims of automation. "The factory, the farms, the mines across the river," Eliot tells his wife Sylvia, "they're almost completely automatic now. And America doesn't even need these people for war—not any more."[17] To love them, on the other hand, poses a more difficult task. Not merely impoverished, the citizens of Rosewater are both morally and physically deficient and, like the sixty-eight year-old virgin, Diana Moon Glampers, "too dumb to live" (70). The "secret thing" that allows Eliot to love these apparently worthless people is, as Sylvia perceives, "that they're human" (67). Indeed, the "main lesson Eliot learned," according to bewhiskered Kilgore Trout, ingenious if unread writer of science fiction, "is that people can use all the uncritical love they can get" (213).[18]

Uncritical love appears unthinkable, however, to those who immediately and vigorously oppose Eliot's mission. Senator Lister Ames Rosewater, Eliot's father, leads this opposition. To receive love, believes the Senator, one first must deserve it. The citizens of Rosewater, he argues, while clearly in need of love and money, deserve neither. "There's absolutely nothing good about ... those people Eliot helps" (66-67), insists the Senator "who hates crooks and weaklings" (174) with equal fervor. Convinced "it's still possible for an American to make a fortune on his own" (105), the Senator holds the unsuccessful responsible for their failure.

Senator Rosewater's convictions reflect two disparate but traditional American attitudes that persevere, if only *sub rosa*, in American thought. The disparaging view Senator Rosewater takes toward the poor and the weak can be seen as part of a mood of Social Darwinism that David L. Bazelon believes still persists in America. Once the primary "rationalization of social irresponsibility," Social Darwinism "has ceased to be intellectually respectable." But, Bazelon goes on to say, "It is not easy for the strong and fortunate to give up the idea that the weak and miserable should be left to their own scant resources,"[19] a conclusion plainly applicable to Senator Rosewater. The Senator's very language reflects this Socially Darwinistic bias. The metaphors he uses to describe the poor contain images often associated with evolutionary theory. Early in the novel, for example, he refers to the citizens of Rosewater as "the maggots in the slime on the bottom of the human garbage pail" (59). While talking to Kilgore Trout near the end of the novel, the Senator asserts his belief that a "poor man with gumption can still elevate himself out of the mire" (210). Such utterances indicate that only time separates Senator Rosewater from predecessors such as William Graham Sumner who championed Social Darwinism on the Senate floor.

The Puritan Ethic more obviously contributes to the Senator's social philosophy. In a way, the Puritan Ethic, with its view of work as almost holy and idleness as "the Devil's workshop," ripened America for Social Darwinism with its emphasis on the necessity for struggle. Both contribute to the belief that hard, honest labor assures social success. When Eliot refers to the "rotten time" had by the poor, Senator Rosewater's reply reveals his faith in the Puritan Ethic. "Perhaps," he answers, "if they ... got to work, they would stop having such a rotten time" (105). He objects to welfare programs, including Eliot's, because he fears what such programs "would do to incentive" (104).

The Senator's sexual prudishness also suggests his Puritan bias. In a hilarious burlesque of the repressive mentality, Vonnegut has Senator Rosewater devise a definition for obscenity. "Obscenity, *it said*, is any picture or phonograph record or any written matter calling attention to reproductive organs, bodily discharges, or bodily hair" (85). The Senator's revulsion at bodily hair receives its funniest treatment when Eliot, emerging from a bath, discovers a foot-long pubic hair and proceeds to uncoil it for his father's approval. The Senator explodes, accuses Eliot of hating him, and storms from Eliot's office.[20]

Faith in the efficacy of honest labor is generally subsumed beneath the rubric, "The American Dream." Using Eliot as his spokesman, Vonnegut makes clear his belief that the dream has failed. In a letter addressed to whoever will succeed Eliot as heir to the Rosewater Foundation, Eliot summarizes the death of that dream. America's founding fathers, Eliot writes, believing the vast and valuable resources of the new continent to be inexhaustible, neglected to limit the wealth of each American citizen. Consequently, "a handful of rapacious citizens," perceiving "that venal office-holders, legislators in particular, could be persuaded to toss up great hunks of [America] for grabs," soon came "to control all that was worth controlling in America" (21). With so much money concentrated in so few hands, the traditional components of the American dream—"hard work and the merit system and honesty" (106)—became useless.

> Thus was the savage and stupid and entirely inappropriate and unnecessary and humorless American class system created. Honest, industrious, peaceful citizens were classed as bloodsuckers, if they asked to be paid a living wage. And they saw that praise was reserved henceforth for those who devised means of getting paid enormously for committing crimes against which no laws had been passed. Thus the American dream turned belly up, turned green, bobbed to the scummy surface of cupidity unlimited, filled with gas, went *bang* in the noonday sun. (21)

Harry Pena of *God Bless You, Mr. Rosewater* represents the best example of the irrelevance of labor and character in a money-mad world. A trap fisherman, Harry must work outdoors because he once inhaled carbon tetrachloride while cleaning his living-room carpet. As portrayed by Vonnegut, Harry "was one of the few men in Pisquontuit [Rhode Island] whose manhood was not in question" (126). Despite his virility, Harry cannot make a living. Ironically, it is Bunny Weeks, wealthy homosexual restaurateur, who most deeply understands the meaning of Harry's impending bankruptcy. "Real people don't make their livings that way any more," Bunny says, referring to Harry's trap fishing. "That's all over, men working with their hands and backs. They are not needed" (151). Harry represents not only the kind of man Bunny can never be, but the kind Bunny does not need to be, nor will need to be ever again. Glancing at "four stupid, silly, fat widows in furs laugh[ing] over a bathroom joke on a paper cocktail napkin," Bunny pronounces what could serve as Harry's and the American dream's epitaph: "And look who's winning. And look who's won" (151).[21]

As persistent and significant aspects of American culture, both the illusions fostered by nationalism and the Great-American-Success-Illusion can be viewed as American institutions. Vonnegut believes the responsibility for such institutionalized illusions rests clearly with Americans. Insofar as he treats these kinds of illusions, Vonnegut engages in social protest.

The second kind of illusion Vonnegut examines lies beyond protest. Whereas the first contributes to human despair and should be discarded, the second helps prevent despair and seems essential to human contentment. This is the illusion of a purposeful universe. Those who embrace it believe the world contains plan, meaning and a moral order, and that in the end all things work for the best. The belief in human progress ties in with this illusion. So long as man believes history unfolds as part of a universal drive toward goodness, he can see his own technological and scientific advances as consistent with this drive, as contributing to a universal goal. Strip purpose from the cosmos, however, and man's confidence collapses. Without a context of universal order and direction, progress seems random and arbitrary. The world, no longer explicable in terms of human reason, becomes unfamiliar, and man—in the words of

Camus—"suddenly deprived of illusions and of light, ... feels a stranger." This dilemma, continues Camus, "truly constitutes the feeling of Absurdity."[22]

Vonnegut's belief in a purposeless universe constitutes his main theme. This theme receives its most extensive treatment in *The Sirens of Titan*.[23] More an extended metaphor for an absurd universe than the science fiction novel it is usually taken to be, *The Sirens of Titan* effectively burlesques the entire notion of purpose in the universe. To be sure, Vonnegut presents a world with purpose, but a purpose stranger than any dreamed of in the philosophies of man.

Set some time "between the Second World War and the Third Great Depression" (8), the novel concerns multi-millionaire Winston Niles Rumfoord, who "had run his private space ship right into the heart of an uncharted chrono-synclastic infundibulum" (13). Rumfoord and his dog Kazak, who had accompanied him in the space ship, find themselves "scattered far and wide, not just through space, but through time, too" (15). As "wave phenomena," they pulse in "distorted spirals with their origins in the Sun and their terminals in Betelgeuse" (266), materializing on any cosmic body that intercepts their spirals.

Rumfoord's circumstances are governed by the inhabitants of Tralfamadore, a planet 150-thousand light years from earth. In fact, every significant historical event on Earth, both past and present, including a Rumfoord-led invasion of Earth by Martians, has been determined by Tralfamadorians. These events form part of a continuous communique from Tralfamadore to Salo, a space-lost Tralfamadorian messenger. Elected to carry a message from "One Rim of the Universe to the Other," Salo experienced space ship trouble enroute and was forced to land on Titan, a tiny planet occupying the same solar system as Earth. After sending a message to Tralfamadore explaining his plight, Salo begins receiving a series of replies. Using a mysterious device called "the Universal Will to Become," the Tralfamadorians influence earthlings to construct these replies to Salo. Stonehenge, for example, means in Tralfamadorian, "Replacement part being rushed with all possible speed" (271). The Great Wall of China means: "Be patient. We haven't forgotten about you" (171). Because the apparatus directing the impulses is often inaccurate, many potential messages go amuck. The decline and fall of great civilizations on earth have been nothing more than communication breakdowns between Tralfamadore and Salo.

The Tralfamadorians use Rumfoord to help get the replacement part to Salo. After various turns of Vonnegut's complicated plot, Salo receives the necessary part and can resume carrying the message that has accounted for all human history. The message is a brief one. "Greetings!" is all it reads. By portraying the whole of human endeavor as nothing more than an exchange of messages between creatures from outer space, Vonnegut effectively debunks beliefs in a purposeful universe, in free will, and in human progress.

These themes recur in Vonnegut's fourth novel, *Cat's Cradle*.[24] Jonah, the novel's protagonist, has decided to write a factual "account of what important Americans had done on the day when the first atomic bomb was dropped on Hiroshima, Japan" (12). He begins gathering information on the late Dr. Felix Hoenikker, "father" of the bomb, whose activities Jonah wishes to include in his book. Jonah does not know that Hoenikker has also invented *ice-nine*, a deadly chemical capable of freezing anything it touches. Jonah's research finally leads him to the island of San Lorenzo, where he converts to Bokononism, a religion that frankly admits its basis in lies. The climax of the novel occurs when, following a bizarre accident, the ice-nine contaminated body of "Papa" Monzano, dictator of San Lorenzo, slides into the ocean, immediately turning the whole world to ice.

Like most of Vonnegut's novels, *Cat's Cradle* can be read on one level as a novel of protest, this time against the destructive powers of science. This is especially evident in Vonnegut's portrait of Felix Hoenikker. The epitome of scientific "objectivity," totally uninterested in people,

Hoenikker remains oblivious to the effects his discoveries may have on mankind. More a naive child than a father of three, Hoenikker treats science as a game; his discoveries, as happy accidents. When a fellow scientist remarks after Hiroshima that science has now known sin, Hoenikker replies, "What is sin?" (21). Through his burlesque-portrait of Hoenikker, Vonnegut voices his concern that science, removed from a context of humanism, posits a danger to humanity. Despite its danger, however, science continues to be unquestionably accepted, even worshiped, in the novel as "magic that works" (143).

But *Cat's Cradle* goes far beyond protest. Like *The Sirens of Titan*, its main comment is upon the futility of human endeavor, the meaninglessness of human existence. This theme is conveyed primarily through the parables and "calypsos" of *The Books of Bokonon*, the Bible of Bokononism written by Bokonon for his followers. A Negro whose real name is Lionel Boyd Johnson, Bokonon was shipwrecked on San Lorenzo with a marine deserter named Earl McCabe. Dreaming of converting San Lorenzo into a Utopia, Johnson and McCabe supplied the island with a new form of government and a new religion. Johnson designed the religion, becoming a self-styled prophet in the process. His "calypso" on the goal of this new religion expresses both the need for the saving lie of religion and the reality of a meaningless universe.

> I wanted all things
> To seem to make some sense
> So we all could be happy, yes,
> Instead of tense.
> And I made up lies
> So that they all fit nice,
> And I made this sad world
> A par-a-dise. (90)

As is always the case in Vonnegut's novels when a strong man tries to help others, McCabe and Johnson fail "to raise the people from misery and muck" (93). Man, Vonnegut repeatedly emphasizes, can seldom help either himself or others. Julian Castle, founder of the House of Hope and Mercy in the Jungle where the ill of San Lorenzo receive free treatment, also discovers this fact. Like McCabe and Johnson, Castle wishes to help the natives. The futility of his wish becomes especially evident when, during a bubonic plague epidemic, Castle ministers to the stricken for days without sleep, saving so few lives that "a bulldozer actually stalled trying to shove [the bodies] toward a common grave" (111). At the height of the epidemic, Castle wanders into the dark and begins shining a flashlight "over all the dead people stacked outside" (112). Turning to his son, who had followed him, Castle giggles, "Son, . . . someday this will all be yours" (112). In this macabre context, the cliché takes on fresh meaning. Despite Castle's efforts, little change will occur. Life will remain "short and brutish and mean" (119).

Bokonon acknowledges this fact in *The Fourteenth Book of Bokonon* entitled "What Can a Thoughtful Man Hope for Mankind on Earth, Given the Experience of the Past Million Years?" The *Book*, one of the shortest in *The Books of Bokonon*, consists of one word and a period: "Nothing" (164). According to both Vonnegut and Bokonon, history is little more than a sequence of absurd events. Moral progress is illusory. From the localized holocaust of Hiroshima man has "progressed" to the world-wide cataclysm of Hoenikker's ice-nine. "History!" writes Bokonon. "Read it and weep!" (168).

Vonnegut's rejection of the idea of human progress reflects the dim view he takes of the human character. This disparaging view of man, along with his belief in a purposeless universe, constitutes Vonnegut's absurdist vision, a vision that overshadows any protest found in his novels. Protest, as indicated in the discussion of *Catch-22*, implies hope for reform. Like most novelists of the absurd, however, Vonnegut entertains little hope for either social or individual reform. Cosmic absurdity informs all things, including man and his institutions. This view of man constitutes a main distinction between Vonnegut's absurdist novels and the novel of radical protest.

Radical protest novels generally view man as the victim of his society. In the protest novels of Dreiser and Steinbeck, for example, a distinction exists between the "decent little people" and the financiers who control conditions. Steinbeck portrays the Joads as decent people who would have remained content cultivating their land had the banks not taken it away from them. Similarly, Dreiser makes it clear that Carrie Meeber's wrongdoings result from the standards of the society in which she finds herself more than from any intrinsic evil in Carrie. As we have seen, Heller's *Catch-22* also portrays potentially decent human beings caught helplessly in the trap of a bureaucracized society. In other words, the social protest novelists could place a certain faith in the masses. The evil these novelists perceive resides in the social system, not in the individual.

For Vonnegut, however, as well as for most contemporary novelists of the absurd, the "little man," while often victimized by a technologically oriented mass society, can seldom attribute his vile, stupid, mean-spirited nature to that society. Whereas the traditional protest novelist believed man would be all right if not for a corrupt social system, Vonnegut views not just man's institutions—but man himself—as absurd.

This theme occurs even in Vonnegut's great anti-utopia novel, *Player Piano*, a novel almost purely of protest. As George Woodcock has indicated, the anti-utopian novel, like the novel of social protest, levels its protest "from the disillusioned left."[25] The difference is that whereas the social protest novel confronts the here and now, the anti-utopia projects a future world. The "fundamental principle" of the latter, to use Mark Hillegas' definition, "is prediction or extrapolation, from existing knowledge and conditions, of things to come."[26] Like the novel of social protest, the anti-utopia "always makes a significant comment on human life: usually it is a vehicle for social criticism and satire."[27] Despite its inclusion in a genre of protest, however, *Player Piano* contains the seeds of Vonnegut's absurdist vision.

Like most anti-Wellsian novels, *Player Piano* takes place in a World State controlled by an elite corps of engineers and managers with the aid of a giant computer, *Epicac XIV*.[28] The mass of men have little to do; most jobs have been taken over by machines. Bored, the masses revolt, but—as in so many Wellsian novels—the revolution fails. Just before their surrender, however, the rebels, whose tactics had involved breaking up the machines in a few cities, begin tinkering with these broken machines, attempting to put them back together again. Vonnegut's irony clearly drives home his point: even had the revolution succeeded, nothing much would have changed. So much for placing one's faith in the masses.

This pessimistic view of human character recurs in *God Bless You, Mr. Rosewater*. Eliot firmly believes that the people to whom he devotes both time and money are "the same sorts ... who, in generations past, had cleared the forests, drained the swamps, built the bridges, people whose sons formed the backbone of the infantry in time of war" (69). Vonnegut makes it clear, however, that Eliot is deluded. "The people who leaned on Eliot regularly were a lot weaker than [Eliot believed]—and dumber, too. When it came time for their sons to go into the Armed Forces, for instance, the sons were generally rejected as being mentally, morally, and physically undesirable" (69-70). Similarly, Felix Hoenikker, the Einstein-like inventor of *Cat's Cradle*, acts independently of any institutions, social or otherwise. Indeed, he is called at one point in the novel "a force of nature no mortal could possibly control" (23).

Even the few figures who display strength of character in Vonnegut's novels do little good and receive no reward for their efforts. The attempts of Bokonon and Julian Castle to help the people of San Lorenzo prove futile, and Harry Pena's virility is simply irrelevant. Similarly, Eliot's ministry not only leaves the bootless citizens of Rosewater unchanged, but Eliot is committed to a mental institution for his efforts.

In the face of such all-encompassing absurdity, what is the proper response for man? Vonnegut offers at least three possible answers to this question. Man may practice uncritical love, hoping through kindness and charity to lend some meaning to an otherwise meaningless human condition. Or he can manufacture new illusions to supplant the old—comforting lies that will shelter him from the icy winds of an absurd universe. Finally, he can simply accept the absurdity of his condition, neither affirming nor denying it and never asking the most meaningless of questions, Why?

Several characters in Vonnegut's novels choose love and kindness as the proper response to life. In *Mother Night*, for example, Howard Campbell, Jr., decides to write a book about the love he and his wife shared. "It was going to show how a pair of lovers in a world gone mad could survive by being loyal only to a nation composed of themselves—a nation of two" (37). Eliot Rosewater also associates love and art. He feels the love he extends to "discarded Americans, even though they're useless and unattractive," serves as his "work of art" (47). Like Eliot, Julian Castle gives up a life of affluent ease to establish his Castle of Hope and Mercy in the jungles of San Lorenzo. Finally, in *The Sirens of Titan*, the lesson is that "a purpose of human life, no matter who is controlling it, is to love whoever is around to be loved" (313).

While Vonnegut's sympathy for this position is obvious, his sympathy never gives way to sentimentality. With the possible exception of *Sirens*, nowhere in his novels does charity bring about any meaningful change. Campbell loves his wife, but she is killed in the war. He then falls in love with his wife's sister, who turns out to be a Russian spy who betrays him. Eliot's charitable activities improve nothing, and Castle's efforts as a doctor fail to alter significantly the high death rate of San Lorenzo. On the one hand, Vonnegut agrees with the "one rule" Eliot Rosewater knows: "God damn it, you've got to be kind" (110). On the other hand, he realizes what is stated in *God Bless You, Mr. Rosewater*, that "the outside world has not been even microscopically improved by the unselfish acts" of man (54).

The acceptance of the futility of human endeavor and the purposelessness of the universe lies beyond the capacity of many. These people need illusions to sustain them. As

Eliot Rosewater tells a psychiatrist in *Slaughterhouse-Five, or the Children's Crusade*, "I think you guys are going to have to come up with a lot of wonderful *new* lies, or people just aren't going to want to go on living."[29] In that same novel, both Eliot and Billy Pilgrim, the novel's protagonist, have "found life meaningless" and are "trying to re-invent themselves and their universe," turning to science-fiction for ideas.

To offset this general sense of meaninglessness, Bokonon erects his religion upon *foma*, harmless untruths. "Man got to tell himself he understand," he asserts in one of his "calypsos" (124). So Bokonon manufactures purpose. One of his lies, for example, states "that humanity is organized into teams . . . that do God's Will without ever discovering what they are doing. Such a team is called a *karass* by Bokonon" (11). Since, as Bokonon says, one is a fool who thinks he sees what God is doing (13), Bokononists should refrain from attempts to fathom the purposes they serve, remaining content with the knowledge that they serve God's ends. *Foma* such as these, says Bokonon, make it possible for man to be "brave and kind and healthy and happy."

Occasionally, however, Bokonon dispels the illusions he perpetrates, as in the following parable.

> In the beginning God created the earth, and he looked upon it in His cosmic loneliness.
>
> And God said, "Let Us make living creatures out of mud, so the mud can see what We have done." And God created every living creature that now moveth, and one was man. Mud as man alone could speak. God leaned close as mud as man sat up, looked around, and spoke. Man blinked. "What is the *purpose* of all this?" he asked politely.
>
> "Everything must have a purpose?" asked God.
>
> "Certainly," said man.
>
> "Then I leave it to you to think of one for all this," said God.
>
> And He went away. (177).

Bokonon's parable exposes the cruel paradox of modern living: "the heartbreaking necessity of lying about reality, and the heartbreaking impossibility of lying about it" (189). Lies, it seems, prove as useless in an absurd universe as charity. The fact of absurdity has become too obvious to conceal.

When both love and lies prove futile as viable responses to the absurd human condition, all that remains—other than suicide—is resignation. True wisdom, Vonnegut implies in *Slaughterhouse-Five*, lies in recognizing the things man cannot change. In the novel Vonnegut also suggests that it would be nice to possess the courage to change the things we can, but the novel offers little indication as to what falls within man's power to reform. "Among the things Billy Pilgrim could not change," for example, "were the past, the present, and the future" (52). The main idea emerging from *Slaughterhouse-Five* seems to be that the proper response to life is one of resigned acceptance.

This resignation undercuts any anti-war sentiment found in the novel. One might as well write an anti-glacier book as an anti-war book, Vonnegut says early in the novel. "And," he continues, "even if wars didn't keep coming like glaciers, there would still be plain old death" (3). In many ways, *Slaughterhouse-Five* is a book about death, an extension of the statement Vonnegut quotes from Celine: "The truth is death" (18). Everytime someone dies in *Slaughterhouse-Five* Vonnegut writes, "So it goes." The phrase occurs over one-hundred times in a one-hundred-eighty-six page novel.

The flippancy of the phrase offers a clue to the effectiveness of *Slaughterhouse-Five*. That effectiveness depends upon the novel's tone, the same kind of tone that colors most of Vonnegut's novels. In these novels, a carefully controlled ironic tension exists between the horrible, often catastrophic, events that make up the content of Vonnegut's novels, on the one hand, and what Richard Schickel calls "the sardonic, unhysteric rationalism of [the narrative] voice" on the other.[30] A second kind of tension also exists in many of his novels. Present in these novels are figures like Julian Castle and Eliot Rosewater, whose concern for humanity contrasts with the absurdity of their surroundings and the hopelessness of the novel's tone. In *Slaughterhouse-Five*, however, no such figure appears. "There are almost no characters in this story," Vonnegut explains, "and almost no dramatic confrontations, because most of the people in it are so sick and so much the listless playthings of enormous forces" (140). So the pervasive hopelessness of the novel's tone remains unmitigated by any character who strives, no matter how futilely, to act in a meaningful manner.

Slaughterhouse-Five is based partially on Vonnegut's own experiences in World War II. Like Vonnegut, Billy Pilgrim is captured by the Germans and taken to Dresden, where he witnesses the destruction of the city by American fire-bombers. While in Germany, Billy first becomes "unstuck in time." For Billy, "all moments, past, present, and future, always have existed, always will exist" (23). "Spastic in time," with "no control over where he is going next," Billy has "seen his birth and death many times, . . . and pays random visits to all the events in between" (20). One of these events involves his kidnaping by Tralfamadorians, who take him via flying saucer to their planet where he lives in a zoo with Montana Wildhack, famous earthling movie star. One of the things the Tralfamadorians teach Billy is that "it is just an illusion we have here on Earth that one moment follows another one, like beads on a string, and that once a moment is gone it is gone forever" (23). True time is like the Rocky Mountains, permanent, and one can "look at any moment that interests [him] " (23).

In *The Sirens of Titan*, Winston Niles Rumfoord possessed the Tralfamadorian ability to view all of time simultaneously. But, as Salo perceives, "even though Rumfoord was chronosynclastic infundibulated, and might be expected to take a larger view of things," he remained "a surprisingly parochial Earthling at heart" (273). Which is to say, Rumfoord could still become upset, even offended, at the absurdity of things. Billy Pilgrim, on the other hand, learns his lessons well from the Tralfamadorians. Completely resigned to the inevitability of events, Billy finds everything "pretty much all right" (135). Even the destruction of Dresden, which claimed the lives of 135,000 German citizens, mostly civilians, draws the following response from Billy: *"Everything is all right, and everybody has to do exactly what he does. I learned that on Tralfamadore"* (171).

The first thing Billy learns from the Tralfamadorians is the utter lack of any cosmic purpose. "Why *you*? Why *us* for that matter? Why *anything*" Billy is told upon being kidnapped. "Because the moment simply is. . . . There is no *why*" (66). One searches for meaning in vain. Time, say the Tralfamadorians, "does not lend itself to warnings or explanations. It simply *is*. Take it moment by moment, and you will find that we are all . . . bugs in amber" (74). The world, in other words, is all that the case is, and attempts either to change or to understand it are foredoomed to failure.

The proper response to life, then, becomes resignation. "God grant me the serenity to accept the things I cannot change" becomes the prayer of relevance, one Vonnegut repeats several times throughout the novel. To enhance this serenity, one should "concentrate on the happy moments of . . . life, and . . . ignore the unhappy ones" (168). Billy succeeds in this advice so well that a fitting epitaph for his tombstone, we are told, might read: "Everything was beautiful, and nothing hurt" (105, 106). This, despite a life filled with such violent events as the destruction of Dresden, his own capture by enemy troops, a plane crash in which his skull is fractured, the bizarre death of his wife by carbon monoxide poisoning, and his eventual assassination by a deranged killer!

Such bland acceptance of "things as they are" seems strange in a Vonnegut novel. Initially, one suspects the novel ridicules rather than recommends such passivity. Yet little in the novel supports this contention. In fact, when Vonnegut suggests the epigraph for Billy Pilgrim, he comments upon its appropriateness to his own life (105). A similar sentiment appears in his introduction to *Welcome to the Monkey House*. The "two main themes of my novels," he writes, "were stated by my siblings."[31] Peter, Vonnegut's older brother, stated the first in a letter home shortly after the birth of his first child. "Here I am," he wrote, "cleaning shit off of practically everything" (xiii). Vonnegut's sister stated the second theme. Dying of cancer, she uttered, "No pain" (xiv). Together, the themes seem contradictory. Can one, aware of how polluted "practically everything" in life has become, remain content with life? Or, to put it another way, why would one able to view painlessly the conditions of life bother to protest those conditions?

The prayer repeated several times in *Slaughterhouse-Five* provides the answer to these questions. "God grant me the serenity," it reads, "to accept the things I cannot change, courage to change the things I can, and wisdom always to tell the difference" (181). Certain things, then, lie within man's control. Included would be those illusions mentioned earlier that make man's life more tedious than necessary, the illusions that contribute to wars and poverty and prejudice. These illusions Vonnegut exposes and ridicules. Most things, however, exceed man's limited control, not to mention his equally limited understanding. True wisdom accepts this fact, acknowledging the lack of universal purpose or meaning or direction. All human activity is blighted by this pervasive absurdity. Since the blight is irremediable, acceptance of it may be the only sane response for man. Indeed, acceptance of absurdity may constitute the only logical extension of the absurdist vision.

The detached tone of Vonnegut's novels is the primary device by which he suggests the hopelessness of the human condition and the resignation he feels is necessary to that hopelessness. As Vonnegut's absurdist vision intensifies with each successive novel, the tone of these novels becomes increasingly "distant." Such "distance" does not suggest "an elaborate novelistic impasse to feeling and judgment," as one critic has maintained.[32] Rather, it indicates Vonnegut's growing resignation to the futility of caring as a viable response in an absurd world. His use of tone constitutes an important part of Vonnegut's absurdist method.

The special use Vonnegut makes of two-dimensional characters also reinforces his absurdist vision. Like Heller,

Vonnegut often uses caricature to burlesque certain ideas and philosophies. Intentionally exaggerated figures such as Senator Rosewater, the Reverend Lionel J. D. Jones, Robert Wilson, and Felix Hoenikker are obvious burlesques of the "ideals" they uphold. Yet Vonnegut does not confine his use of two-dimensional characters to satire. In fact, he seldom depicts a "well-rounded" character at all. Almost none of his characters actually develops in the course of the novels.

We know many facts about the life of Eliot Rosewater, for example. We know that he was born in 1918 in Washington, D.C., that he spent much of his boyhood on the Eastern seaboard and in Europe, that he likes to sail and to ski, and that after a brief period at Harvard Law School he enlisted in the infantry, distinguished himself in many battles, and rose to the rank of captain before suffering combat fatigue near the war's end. We also know that while hospitalized in Europe he met and married Sylvia, his nurse, and then returned to Harvard where he earned his law degree and an eventual Ph.D. in international law. We know he was partially responsible for the death of his mother in a boating accident and that while in Europe he accidentally bayoneted two old men and a fourteen-year-old boy whom he mistook for German soldiers. Each of these facts, however, is merely stated. They in no wise contribute to the development of Eliot's character, which remains rather "flat" and two-dimensional; nor do they aid in our understanding of his actions. We never know, for example, why he goes to Rosewater, Indiana. "His Destination is there" (58), we are told—which does not adequately explain Eliot's motivation.[33]

Eliot leaves Rosewater as suddenly and as mysteriously as he arrived. Again, no clear motivation is provided. Dr. Ed Brown, the young psychiatrist who treats Sylvia when she suffers her breakdown, supplies as good an explanation as any. Eliot left Rosewater because he contracted Samaritrophia, defined by Brown as "hysterical indifference to the troubles of those less fortunate than oneself" (54). The disease, which attacks only "those exceedingly rare indi-

viduals who reach biological maturity still loving and want-
ing to help their fellow man" (56), occurs when the conscience is overthrown by the rest of the mind. Brown's
prognosis is absurd, of course; but its explanation of Eliot's
actions is as valid as a more "scientific" diagnosis would
be—which is to say, not valid at all.

The point of Vonnegut's burlesque is that human actions
do not always correspond to readily ascertainable motives.
The belief that human actions proceed from certain sociological and psychological causes and that these responses
can be measured and even predicted, simply constitutes another illusion man has erected to block out the reality of a
directionless and chaotic universe. Vonnegut's reluctance to
depict well-developed characters and to supply them with
conventional motives for their actions serves as a conscious
burlesque of the whole concept of realism in the novel. As
Robert Scholes has pointed out, novelists of the past century or so have assumed that "a readily ascertainable thing
called reality exists and that we all live in it." Thus, reality
became "the only thing to write about."[34] This realism
extended to characters; consequently, the humorous caricatures common to eighteenth- and nineteenth-century novels
gave way to the well-developed, "round" characters of the
modern novel—characters who were "psychologically valid."
Vonnegut rejects all formulations of reality, whether they
be religious, philosophical, scientific, or literary. Psychology
is simply another delusive attempt to explain and systema-
tize the inexplicable and chaotic, for man is as absurd as
his universe. The well-rounded character whose actions proceed from clearly stated causes, then, represents a falsification. By peopling his novels with oversimplified, two-dimensional figures, Vonnegut mocks the belief that human
beings can be understood in all their chaotic complexity,
much less captured on the printed page.[35]

From the standpoint of both craft and theme, Kurt Vonnegut, Jr., must be reckoned a serious artist. His novels
have progressed from satire to absurdity, from the early
protest of *Player Piano* to the almost total resignation of
Slaughterhouse-Five. Accompanying the gradual intensifica-

tion of his absurdist vision has been an increased use of innovative techniques that reinforce that vision. Though Vonnegut's angle of vision has become increasingly absurdist, it remains steadfastly comic. Never does he give way to despair or empty cynicism. He has managed to face the absurdity of the human condition squarely without losing his concern for humanity or his sense of humor. Perhaps the comment Vonnegut makes most consistently in his novels is best summed up by Bokonon. "Maturity," Bokonon tells us, "is a bitter disappointment for which no remedy exists, unless laughter can be said to remedy anything" (134). The sincerity of his vision and the skill with which he handles his materials rank Kurt Vonnegut, Jr., among the more significant contemporary American novelists of the absurd.

IV

Death and Absurdity:
Thomas Pynchon and the Entropic Vision

PERHAPS more than any other traditional factor, the awareness of death has contributed to the feelings of meaninglessness and anxiety that partly constitute the sense of the absurd. Leo Tolstoy, in chronicling the *Angst* that gripped him during middle-age, links death with absurdity:

> The truth was that life was meaningless. Every day of life, every step in it, brought me, as it were, nearer the precipice, and I saw clearly that before me there was nothing but ruin. And to stop was impossible; to go back was impossible; and it was impossible to shut my eyes so as not to see that there was nothing before me but suffering and actual death, absolute annihilation.[1]

Jean Paul Sartre also associates death and meaninglessness. In "The Wall" he expresses his idea that the ridiculous and arbitrary termination of human life makes life itself similarly ridiculous and arbitrary. And the prayer uttered by the old waiter at the end of Hemingway's "A Clean, Well-Lighted Place" gives chilling expression to the void sensed by the man who lives his life against a backdrop of utter and irrevocable annihilation.

Thomas Pynchon, the youngest of the novelists treated in this study, also chooses death as a major theme. The death that interests him, however, extends beyond the demise of individuals. Pynchon's concern is with cosmic decay, the running down of time as we know it—the death, in short, of the universe. His preoccupation with such large-scale disintegration represents a peculiarly modern phenomenon. Before the study of heat, as Hans Meyerhoff has noted, classical mechanics saw time as directionless. Man might die, but time marched perpetually onward. According to the teachings of modern physics, however, particularly that area of thermodynamics concerned with entropy, time moves irreversibly "towards death."[2]

Entropy refers to the gradual leveling of energy in the universe. In any isolated system—whether that system be a steam engine or a man, a galaxy or a culture—entropy, in keeping with the second law of thermodynamics, tends to increase. As entropy increases, the system draws closer to chaos, its most probable state. For the improbability of any system—whether biological, sociological, or mechanical—exists in proportion to the complexity of its arrangement, system patterns, and structure.[3] As the distribution of energy becomes more uniform, says mathematician Norbert Wiener, "the universe and all closed systems in the universe, tend naturally to deteriorate and lose their distinctiveness, to move from the least to the most probable state, from a state of organization and differentiation in which distinctions and forms exist, to a state of chaos and sameness."[4] Energy in the universe will continue its leveling process until a state of total equilibrium is reached. In this final state of uniformity, heat energy will be non-transferable, since every point will contain the same quantity of energy. All things will be at the same temperature, all matter will be evenly distributed, and nothing more can happen. Such is the "heat-death" most scientists agree will ultimately consume the universe.

In his novels, Pynchon translates the entropic process into social terms. As Pynchon sees him, man—like his universe—undergoes continuous decay. He is destroyed on the one hand by all the accidents and natural disasters flesh is heir to, what Pynchon calls a "succession of encounters between groups of living and a congruent world which simply doesn't care," as well as by a repetition of wars, crises,

and riots. On the other hand, the conforming sameness of
modern organization man reflects symptomatically the state
of de-differentiation Pynchon believes is becoming increasingly characteristic of our universe. A form of disintegration more subtle than these is the dehumanizing processes
of a mechanistic society that transform animate man into
inanimate automaton. Pynchon's concern with a deteriorating humanity constitutes what may be called his entropic
vision.

An early example of this vision occurs in "Entropy," a
significantly entitled short story.[5] Callistro, a character in
the story, is a fifty-four-year-old student of thermodynamics obsessed with the prospect of "heat-death." Like
Pynchon, Callistro has found "in entropy ... an adequate
metaphor to apply to certain phenomena in his own world"
(283). He sees proof all around him of an encroaching
chaos. In what he calls the "consumerism" of Wall Street,
for example, Callistro finds a "tendency ... from differentiation to sameness, from ordered individuality to a kind of
chaos" (283-84). To escape this deterioration, he has converted his apartment into a hothouse, filling it with birds,
plants, and art objects. Hermetically sealed from the outside world, the apartment constitutes "a tiny enclave of
regularity in the city's chaos, alien to the vagaries of the
weather, of national politics, of any civil disorder" (279).
Sharing this enclave is Aubade, Callistro's mistress, who also
struggles against chaos to preserve the "architectonic purity" of their world.

In the apartment below, a party rages. Up through the
floor of Callistro's apartment filter sounds of music and
raucous laughter, "hints of anarchy" that threaten the
"ecological balance" of his hothouse world. When a group
of sailors mistake the apartment where the party is being
held for a whorehouse, a fight breaks out, seeming to inten-
sify the chaotic conditions outside Callistro's "enclave."
Adding to Callistro's concern is his awareness that the temperature outside has remained a steady 37-degrees for the
past three days. Fearful that the temperature equilibrium
known as the "heat-death" has arrived, Aubade breaks the

window that separates their apartment from the outside, and, yielding themselves to the inevitable, Aubade and Callistro await the moment "when 37-degrees Farenheit should prevail both outside and inside, and forever . . ." (292).

Pynchon's concern with disintegration is repeated in *V.*, his first novel, for which he received the Faulkner First Novel Award in 1963. *V.* has a complicated structure, displays a variety of literary styles, and ranges in its five-hundred pages over half-a-century and several continents. In writing it, Pynchon made use of many of the devices discussed in previous chapters. Involuted chronology, comic chapter headings, two-dimensional characters with funny names, to cite a few, comprise the familiar techniques that appear in the novel. His basic technique, however, is the use of entropy as a central metaphor. This metaphor merges so completely with events in the novel that form and theme finally become inextricable. Indeed, the novel stands as a kind of extended metaphor, an elaborate symbol, for the entropic process on the one hand and—to a lesser degree—for the quantum theory on the other.

Quantum physics began in 1899 when Max Planck discovered the discontinuous nature of energy. Energy, Planck found, exists in units or "quanta" that cannot be adequately described by any measuring device of classical physics. "For example," explains Jacob Bronowski, "the more accurately we try to measure the position of a fundamental particle, of an electron say, the less certain will we be of its speed. The more accurately we try to eliminate its speed, the more uncertain will we be of its precise position. Therefore we can never predict the future of the particle with complete certainty; because as a matter of fact we cannot be completely certain of its present."[6] Since all things contain what German physicist Werner Heisenberg calls "the principle of uncertainty," man's knowledge becomes irreducibly inaccurate. Uncertainty becomes the rule, never the exception.

Such uncertainty forms a predominant characteristic of *V.* Like the scientist who attempts to describe a "quanta" of energy, the reader of Pynchon's novel can never be sure of exactly what he sees. Part of this uncertainty results from the ambiguous manner in which the novel is narrated. Action in the novel is divided into seven time blocks: the "present," 1955-56, which takes place largely in New York City; 1898 in Alexandria and Cairo; 1899 in Florence, Italy; 1922 in Southwest Africa; 1937-43 in Valletta, Malta; 1913 in Paris; and 1919, also in Malta. Eleven of the novel's seventeen chapters occur in the "present," develop chronologically, and are related by an omniscient narrator. The narrator refuses however, to remain the usual "disembodied voice," occasionally addressing the reader directly. After itemizing a number of disasters, for example, the narrator directs the reader to confirm the facts just presented: "Look in any yearly Almanac, under 'Disasters'— which is where the figures above come from."[7] As John W. Hunt indicates, "Such passages indicate that what we are being given here is something in the nature of a report, an attempt to put data before us from any and all points of view by a narrator who refuses commitment to any specific meaning or set of meanings the material might suggest."[8] Such narrative reluctance, combined with the direct address, endows the narrator with personality, fleshes him out, as it were. Consequently, the narrator becomes another character in the novel, one whose reluctance to draw connections between the incidents he reports makes more difficult the reader's efforts to discover the novel's "statement."

Most of the remaining time blocks are ordered by the mind of Herbert Stencil, central figure in one of the three plots that thread their way through *V*. When Stencil discovered an entry in his father's journal that referred to a mysterious V., he began his quest for the meaning of V. The "past-tense" sections of the novel involve his discoveries as well as certain clues to the true meaning of V. that remain unknown to Stencil. The uncertainty of these sections results from Stencil's methods of investigation. Not only does he roam the world collecting information concerning V.'s identity, but he supplements this gathered information with what Pynchon calls "impersonation and

dream" (63). "Around each seed of a dossier," writes
Pynchon, "had developed a nacreous mass of inference,
poetic license, forcible dislocation of personality into a past
he didn't remember and had no right in, save the right of
imaginative anxiety or historical care, which is recognized
by no one" (62). In Chapter Three, for example, Stencil
projects himself into the role of eight imaginary characters
who witness the activities of Victoria Wren, a likely candi-
date for V., in Alexandria and Cairo in 1898. Given such
"impersonation," the reader—who becomes as involved in
the search for V. as Stencil—can never be certain which
facts are reliable and which are merely products of Stencil's
imagination. Even those chapters only indirectly concerned
with Stencil, such as Kurt Mondaugen's recounting of the
"Siege-Party" in Southwest Africa, undergo "considerable
change" when retold by Stencil, "become ... Stencilized"
(228).

The uncertainty that results from this narrative ambi-
guity has prompted John W. Hunt to call *V.* a novel of
"anti-vision." According to Hunt, "what is *seen* in Pynchon's [novel] is deliberately obscured rather than illumi-
nated. ..."[9] This obscurity especially applies to the letter
"V," the novel's central symbol. In his quest for its meaning, Stencil encounters small difficulty finding possible
referents. To the contrary, he encounters a multiplicity of
possibilities. Hunt provides the following partial list of
possible V's: " ... Victoria, Vera, Veronica, but also Valletta on the island of Malta, as well as Vesuvius and Venezuela; and the mysterious letter seems also to stand for the
'V' of perspective lines made by lights on a receding street,
the 'V' of spread thighs or of migratory birds; it is the
V-note, where the Whole Sick Crew listens to jazz, as well
as Veronica the sewer rat, the Venus of Botticelli, the Virgin Mother, and the *mons Veneris*. There is even the suggestion, but no clear evidence, that V. is Stencil's own mother."[10] Since in terms of the novel V. comes to represent, if
not truth, then some clue to its ultimate nature, these man-
ifold references suggest that the essential nature of truth is
one of boundless multiplicity. Its essence is uncertainty.

The novel suggests more about the nature of reality than its multiplicity, however. "Events," Stencil notices as his quest brings him closer to the truth about V., "seem to be ordered into an ominous logic" (449). His perception of this sinister order causes Stencil to adopt an "approach and avoid" strategy in his search for the elusive V. He obviously senses what has also become clear to the reader—that almost every referent of V. in the novel touches in some way upon disintegration. In fact, the letter finally comes to serve as an emblem for the entropic process itself. Entropy is the "ultimate Plot Which Has No Name" (226), the truth which lies hidden in the "grand Gothic pile of inferences" (226) Stencil has amassed from "the rathouse of history's rags and straws" (225).

The first V. seen in the novel suggests entropy. Standing on East Main in Norfolk, Virginia, Benny Profane, whose aimless wanderings constitute another of the novel's plots, notices mercury-vapor lamps overhead, their green light "receding in an asymmetric V to the east where it's dark and there are no more bars" (10). In both shape and significance, the lamps suggest Jacob Bronowski's comparison of the future to a stream of gas shot from a nozzle. The farther the gas jet is propelled, the more diffuse become its molecules. Likewise, as time progresses, our system becomes less organized and its structure more and more random. Like the green V's of the lamps Benny perceives on East Main, time propels itself inexorably onward toward darkness and inertia.

Victoria Wren, whose activities over a forty-five year period comprise the novel's third major plot, represents the most significant of the novel's many V's. Some time in 1899, the year Sidney Stencil, Herbert's father, is seduced by Victoria in Florence, Sidney wrote in his journal the sentences which motivate Herbert's search: "There is more behind and inside V. than any of us had suspected. Not who, but what: what is she. God grant that I may never be called upon to write the answer, either here or in any official report" (53). In the ensuing chapters, Pynchon sets out to show that Victoria embodies the entropic process itself.

Her activities as spy contribute to the wars that destroy man. But more significant is her progression toward becoming "intimate," as Pynchon phrases it, "with the things in the Back Room" (410), a bodily accumulation of all that is inanimate.

Her progression toward the inanimate covers forty-five years and involves several identities. She first appears in Egypt in 1898 as an eighteen-year-old convent dropout. Young Victoria meets several agents of the British foreign service, has an affair with one of them (Goodfellow), and finally aids in the assassination of another, Porpentine, whose crime is that he had begun to care about human beings, something a spy must never do. "But someday, Porpentine," he is warned by Bongo-Shaftsbury, another agent, "I, or another, will catch you off guard. Loving, hating, even showing some absent-minded sympathy. . . . The moment you forget yourself enough to admit another's humanity, see him as a person and not a symbol—then perhaps" (81). By helping kill Porpentine for the "crime" of human sympathy, Victoria begins her own removal from the magnetic chain of human sympathy.

She next appears in Florence as a high-priced nineteen-year-old prostitute who rationalizes her illicit affairs by viewing each lover as an "imperfect, mortal version" of Christ, whom she "married" while still a novice. Involved as well in diplomatic intrigue, she spies purely for the sake of whatever skill or virtu' is required, a skill which "became more effective the further divorced it was from moral intention" (198). V.'s next appearance, in order of chronology, is at Paris in 1913, where at age thirty-three she is becoming aware of "her own progression toward inanimateness" (410). A patroness of the theater, V. collects young dancers, who, to satisfy her fetish, are treated as "inanimate objects of desire" (411). In 1919, she next appears in Malta as thirty-nine-year-old Veronica Manganese, now fully involved in even the cruelest aspects of international diplomatic intrigue. Her progression toward inanimateness becomes further heightened, for she has an artificial eye, complete with a clock-iris, and a star sapphire sewn into her navel. If in Paris she treated human beings as objects, now, "obsessed with bodily incorporating little bits of inert matter" (488), she attempts to become an inanimate object herself. After turning up at Foppl's Siege Party in Southwest Africa as forty-two-year-old Vera Meroving, V. makes her final appearance in Valletta. As an inverted priest, she teaches nihilism to the children of Malta, advising the girls to become nuns and the boys to seek the sterile "immortality of rock" (340). Her death at sixty-three reveals how far her progression toward the inanimate had gone. Trapped beneath a fallen pillar, she is literally disassembled by the children, who first strip away her false hair (revealing a tattooed skull beneath), then her clock-iris eye, her teeth, even her foot and leg, fashioned from gold. Dead, V. has become "one with the inanimate universe" (410), her progression toward inertia complete.

Pynchon defines such a "clear movement toward death, or, preferably, non-humanity" as decadence (321, 405). By becoming more and more inanimate, men move "closer to the time when like any dead leaf or fragment of metal they'd be finally subject to the law of physics" (321). So long as man retains his essentially human nature, he can temporarily resist the general stream of corruption and decay in the universe. Norbert Wiener calls such resistance "homeostasis." Through this process, "certain organisms, such as man, tend for a time to maintain and often even to increase the level of their organization, as a local enclave in the general stream of increasing entropy, of increasing chaos and de-differentiation."[11] In proportion to the increase of his inanimateness, however, man moves farther and farther from the homeostatic state. In seeking to become inanimate, he seeks death. Thus Freud's death wish becomes what Freud himself called a kind of "psychical entropy."[12] Just as the entropic loss of structure in our system can be defined, in the words of Wylie Sypher, as its "tendency to sink back into that original chaos from which it may have emerged,"[13] so the Freudian death wish may be seen as a subconscious desire to return to the inorganic state from which man arose.[14] It is this desire to achieve an inert state that motivates V.'s obsession with the in-animate.

Not only V. seeks death in the novel, however. In her bizarre relationship with V., Melanie, the young Parisian ballerina, certainly serves as V.'s fetish, but—possessed of a perverse love for her own mirror-image—she becomes her own fetish as well (410). Such fetishism, Pynchon states, represents an attempt to establish the "Kingdom of Death" on earth (411). Melanie moves to the logical conclusion of fetish worship when, in one of the novel's most horrifying scenes, she impales herself on a pointed stake while per-forming the ballet finale of "The Rape of the Chinese Vir-gins" (412-14).[15]

Likewise, the alligators hunted by Profane beneath the streets of New York seek death. Purchased as toys and then flushed down toilets when tired of, the alligators have wearied of being mere "consumer-objects." They allow Benny to catch and shoot them, for they desire "to go back to what they'd been; and the most perfect shape of that was dead . . ." (146). Others in the novel are found in various stages of inanimation. Bongo-Shaftsbury, the in-humane agent who refers to himself as an "electro-mechani-cal doll," has a miniature electric switch sewn into his arm (80). Fergus-Mixolydian, his counterpart of sixty years later, has placed two electrodes "on the inner skin of his forearm" which, connected to the switch on his television set, turn it off whenever Fergus falls asleep. "Fergus thus became an extension of the TV set" (56). There is also Shale Shoenmaker, the plastic surgeon, whose dedication to the repair of those damaged by the inanimate deteriorates until he eventually falls in "alignment with the inanimate" himself (101), treating his patients as mere objects that need fixing.

Even Benny Profane, the novel's protagonist, who osten-sibly is in flight from the inanimate, may, as Herbert Sten-cil suggests about himself, seek "his own extermination" (451).[16] On the one hand, Benny constantly bumps into trash cans and coke machines, narrowly escapes being squeezed between subway doors, trips on discarded tin

cans, and is generally beleaguered on all sides by the inanimate. A *schlemihl*, "he'd known for years" that "inanimate
objects and he could not live in peace" (37). Yet much in
the novel suggests that Benny also possesses an ambivalent
desire for annihilation. His "pissing at the sun" in an attempt to "put it out for good and all" (26) certainly
smacks of nihilism, as does his "Angel of Death" routine,
during which he marks "the doors of tomorrow's victims"
not with blood but with contraceptives, obvious symbols of
sterility (29). His perception of the alligator's death wish
could be a subconscious projection of his own desire to die.
Moreover, his dream that the various parts of his body fall
apart when a Golden Screw is removed from his navel
(39-40) not only foreshadows the disassembling of the Bad
Priest in Chapter Eleven, but may be wish fulfillment. Benny suspects this possibility himself, as he wonders if his
return to New York City is similar to an elephant's return
to "his graveyard" (40). Finally, his constant evasion of
any emotional involvement with other human beings suggests that he partakes, to a degree, of the very inanimateness he eschews. His refusal to relieve Fina of her sexual
frustrations results in her submission to a "gang-bang" by
the Playboys. He also refuses the advances of Paola Maijstral, a young girl from Malta; and, blaming his schlemihl-
hood, he deserts Rachel Owlglass as well. Rachel's assess-
ment of him is for the most part valid:

> "You are scared of love and all that means is somebody else.
> ... As long as you don't have to give anything, be held to
> anything, sure: you can talk about love. Anything you have to
> talk about isn't real. It's only a way of putting yourself up.
> And anybody who tried to get through to you—me—down."
> (383)

Profane's decisions to save Paola from the sexual assault
of Pig Bodine, his animalistic shipmate, and to help make
possible her later reunion with Pappy Hod, her husband,
indicate some feelings of responsibility. But his ambivalence
remains unresolved, and he can say with honesty as the
novel ends that from his experiences he has not "learned a
goddam thing" (454).

Another V. used by Pynchon in developing his entropic vision is Vhiessu. In a parody of the foreign intrigue genre, Pynchon has various secret agents interpret Vhiessu as a code-name for Venezuela or Vesuvius. Its true meaning, however, is more sinister. For beneath the multi-colored "skin" of Vhiessu, located deep in the African jungle, famous explorer Hugh Godolphin discovered a "hard dead-point of truth" so similar to that which lies "below the glittering integument of every . . . land" that it "can be phrased in identical words" (184). This truth, which finds its concrete embodiment in the Antarctic wasteland, is final and ultimate annihilation. At the core of earth's reality lies "Nothing" (204). Godolphin's obsession with Vhiessu, he realizes with awe, is actually an obsession with death, a "dream of annihilation" (206). After hearing Godolphin's story, Mantissa, the revolutionary turned thief, realizes that his obsession with securing Botticelli's "Birth of Venus" reflects his own sublimated death wish. "Yet she [the Venus] was no less Rafael Mantissa's entire love" (210).

Even the various "Situations" in the novel, as Sidney Stencil realizes, have no "objective reality" but exist only in "the minds of those who happened to be in on it at any specific moment" (189). Diplomatic people "are living al-ways on the verge of some precipice or other," the Gaucho, professional revolutionary, tells Evan Godolphin, Hugh's son. "Without a crisis they wouldn't be able to sleep nights" (193). These crises, it seems, are but sublimations of the same nihilistic dream that motivates Godolphin and Mantissa. But these sublimations relate more closely to what actually is desired, for any crisis has the potential to plunge the world into apocalypse (193-94).

Indeed, the implication seems to be that all history is but a frenzied pursuit of a nihilistic dream, that down the ravaged corridors of time man has chased his own destruc-tion, and that with each successive crisis, each increasingly devastating war, man comes one step closer to the apoca-lypse he seeks. To portray this historical death-drift Pynchon includes in *V.* a host of crises, riots, and sieges. A partial list includes the Fashoda crisis, the Suez crisis, the riots in Florence and Malta, the siege of Khartoum, the siege of the native Bondels in Southwest Africa, the Christmas Siege of Fiume in 1920, and the bombing of Malta in World War II. Such incidents, Pynchon indicates, are perpetual. Symptomatic of man's death wish on a large scale, they are merely one aspect of the continuing universal entropic process.

In 1919 Stencil comments that the public sees World War I as "a new and rare disease which has now been cured and conquered for ever" (461). But war, says Mehemet, the hashish-smoking skipper, is symptomatic not of disease but of old age. The "body slows down, machines wear out, planets falter and loop, sun and stars gutter and smoke." To call war a disease in the face of such natural evidence to the contrary is simply "to bring it down to a size you can look at and feel comfortable . . ." (461). Reflecting upon the millions killed and wounded in World War I, Sidney Stencil refuses to see the holocaust as a "sudden prodigy sprung on a world unaware" (459). The war should have been expected, he insists, for it represented "no innovation, no special breach of nature, or suspension of familiar principles. If it came as any surprise to the public then their own blindness is the Great Tragedy, hardly the war itself" (457).

Perhaps the most horrifying example of these violent incidents is Foppl's description of the Rebellion of 1904-07 in Southwest Africa. Under General Lothar von Trotha, who was sent by Germany to put down the rebellious Hererots and Hottentots, some 60,000 natives were slaughtered, a statistic, remarks Pynchon as he alludes to a more recent case of genocide, that "is only 1 per cent of six million, but still pretty good" (245). Pynchon is at his graphic best in describing the horrors of the siege: the death march of the Hottentot prisoners from Warmbad to Keetmanshoop (261-64), the mass rape of Sarah, a Herero child, by an entire platoon of German soldiers, and the following brief but terrifying description of another child-rape:

Later, toward dusk, there was one Herero girl, 16 or 17 years old, for the platoon; and Fire-lily's rider [Foppl] was last. After he'd had her he must have hesitated a moment between sidearm and bayonet. She actually smiled then; pointed to both, and began to shift her hips lazily in the dust. He used both. (264)

Foppl tells his gory tale during the Siege Party in 1922, a party that dissolves into drunkenness, sadism, and sexual perversion while, outside, another purge of the natives occurs. Similar decadence had been witnessed years before by Kurt Mondaugen at the Fasching in Munich, and it reminds him of the Dance of Death (243-44). But such decadence, he feels, has now spread: "This was a soul-depression which must surely infest Europe as it infested this house" (277).

Such "soul-depression" occurs in New York thirty-four years later as the Whole Sick Crew engage in a continuous *danse macabre* of their own (296).[17] The Crew's favorite saying is "Why not?" and their favorite sport is "yo-yoing," drifting aimlessly from one spot, usually a party, to another. Their activities are as random and directionless as the universe becomes in its steady progress toward final equilibrium.

Epitomizing this decadence is Slab, a "Catatonic Expressionist" who considers his art "the ultimate in non-communication" (56). The painting representing his "revolt against Catatonic Expressionism," however, most obviously portrays man's entropic drift toward chaos. The painting depicts a Partridge in a Pear Tree, Slab's replacement for the Cross as a universal symbol. Animate, yet working "like a machine," the partridge derives nourishment from the pear tree which is in turn nourished by the bird's droppings. The result is "perpetual motion," a perfect state of homeostasis. In one corner of the painting, however, awaits a gargoyle, the point of whose largest fang "lay on an imaginary line projected parallel to the axis of the tree and drawn through the head of the bird" (282). As the tree grows, the bird's head will rise progressively toward eventual impalement on the gargoyle's teeth. Though Slab denies allegory, the symbolism is blatantly clear. Man, like the partridge, is capable of homeostasis, but he moves toward chaos nonetheless. Like the bird, he is too stupid to "fly away" from imminent destruction. "He used to know how to fly once," says Slab, "but he's forgotten" (283).

Pynchon portrays two basic responses to this death drift. Under what he terms The Street, Pynchon subsumes organized religion, political activism, the two-dimensional world of tourism (408-9), and the desperate frivolity of East Main and the Whole Sick Crew. The Street, which Pynchon associates with the political left, includes all the inadequate "social" alternatives to decay that involve "manipulated mob violence" (468) and regimentation. It includes as well the Crew's mindless search for novelty in a world rapidly losing all differentiations. Thus, the entropic homogenization of the physical world finds its social equivalent in the various aspects of The Street.

Just as the goals of The Street exist always in "the dreamscape of the future" (468), so the goals of The Hothouse—what Pynchon terms the second response—are based on a fraudulent sense of the past. "This is the world of the private, isolated soul," writes Don Hausdorff, "insatiably amassing inanimate things, whether of money, ritual, or memory."[18] Callistro's hermetic enclave, Fausto II's retreat into religious abstraction (315-16), Sidney Stencil's nostalgic attachment to Florence—"It could be the age's worst side-effect: nostalgia" (488)—Godolphin's obsession with Vhiessu, each of these is in some respect a version of the Hothouse response. Such flights of nostalgia are futile, for as Sir Edmund Whittaker says, "The cosmos is a one-way system, in which the restoration of a past state of things is impossible: The world moves steadily onward to its doom."[19] Absent in both responses, as Sidney Stencil realizes, is any commitment to the "real present" (468).[20]

Certain characters in V. do commit themselves to the present, however. These characters, who resist the inexorable drift toward chaos, embody Pynchon's emergent value. For despite his awareness that "the only change is toward death" (460), Pynchon ultimately dissociates himself from pessimism. He remains at one with Norbert Wiener, who, after acknowledging the fact of entropy in *The Human Use of Human Beings*, writes:

> In a very real sense we are shipwrecked passengers on a doomed planet. Yet even in a shipwreck, human decencies and human values do not necessarily vanish, and we must make the most of them. We shall go down, but let it be in a manner to which we may look forward as worthy of our dignity.[21]

Like Wiener, Pynchon agrees that we must continue "painting the side of [our] sinking ship" (460).

An early character embodying Pynchon's emergent value is Meatball Mulligan, who owns the apartment below Callistro where the party takes place in the short story "Entropy." When the fight breaks out, Meatball must determine what to do about it. He considers hiding in the closet, but decides that inside would be "dark and stuffy" and that he would be alone. Unlike Callistro, whose apartment became a kind of closet to hide in, Meatball "did not feature being alone" (291). Besides, the chaos outside the closet was likely to come in, for the "crew off the good ship Lollipop or whatever it was might take it upon themselves to kick down the closet door, for a lark" (291). He decides to try and stop the fight. This way, "to try and keep . . . his party from deteriorating into total chaos," is "more a pain in the neck, but probably better in the long run" (291).

In *V.* characters like Meatball who refuse to "drift into the graceful decadence of an enervated fatalism" ("Entropy," p. 283) include Rachel Owlglass, who is devoted to aiding the world's "victims," Paola Maijstral, who is able to love, and Paola's father, Fausto, who manages to turn away from a state of inanimateness toward one of humanity. There is also McClintic Sphere, black jazz musician, who somewhat obtrusively delivers the novel's coda: "Love with your mouth shut, help without breaking your ass or publicizing it; keep cool, but care" (365-66). Pockets of organization in an otherwise ubiquitous chaos, these characters do care. And that, Pynchon insists, matters.

As Don Hausdorff points out, Malta, the Rock, stands as a sort of homeostatic symbol. A "clinched fist" to which most of the novel's "yo-yos" return, Malta has suffered the senseless and devastating power of Nazi bombers, yet it somehow has managed survival. Its attributed qualities— "invincibility, tenacity, perseverance" (325)—are less metaphor than delusion. "But on the strength of this delusion Malta survived" (325). In other words, Malta, like man, will eventually succumb to the laws of thermodynamics, although, like "the tough old earth," it will probably "take its own time in dying," crumbling finally of "old age" (461). In the meantime, regardless of the absurdity of all actions in a universe doomed to disintegration, man must attempt to prevent entropy. Although such attempts are foredoomed to failure, the delusion that disintegration can be resisted results in a humanism that, if desperate, is, Pynchon believes, nonetheless necessary.

So far the kind of entropy discussed belongs to thermodynamics, the study of heat. Cybernetics, the science of communications, also deals with entropy, but relates it to the order and disorder of messages. Messages, "themselves a form of pattern and organization,"[22] afford man one method for achieving a degree of order in a world tending to disorder. "But as efficient as communications mechanisms become," writes Norbert Wiener, a pioneer in the field of Cybernetics, "they are still, as they have always been, subject to the overwhelming tendency for entropy to increase, for information to leak in transit. . . ."[23] Pynchon's knowledge of information theory is evident in "Entropy." When Saul and his girl quarrel, Meatball suggests that their problem is semantic, "a language barrier." Saul, who knows his Cybernetics, replies:

> No, ace, it is *not* a barrier. If it is anything it's a kind of leakage. Tell a girl: "I love you." No trouble with two-thirds of that, it's a closed circuit. Just you and she. But that nasty four-letter word in the middle, *that's* the one you have to look out for. Leakage. All that is noise. Noise screws up your signal, makes for disorganization in the circuit. (285)

Something like the homeostatic state is achieved in communications when the entropic "leakage" Saul complains of is resisted and an adequate exchange of information results. Such successful exchanges constitute a process by which human beings temporarily resist the general stream of corruption and disorganization in the universe.

One way man uses information to improve himself and his society involves a process called "feedback." Inherent in the very structure of the human organism are what Wiener calls variety and possibility. Feedback occurs when man, as a result of these qualities, derives information from "past experiences," then modifies his "pattern of behavior into one which in some sense or the other will deal more effectively with the future environment."[24] Yet, Wiener continues, modern mass society deprives man of his capability to respond variously to experience by organizing him into a kind of ant-state. The "worshipers of efficiency" who control mass society, complains Wiener, "would like to have each man move in a social orbit meted out to him from his childhood, and perform a function to which he is bound as the serf was bound to the clod."[25]

Elaborating upon Wiener's views, psychoanalyst Erich Fromm says that in a capitalistic society not only goods, but human skills and energy, become commodities. Since the owner of capital buys labor to produce goods that have a marketable demand, so must the laborer produce in accord with these demands or starve. Hence, both goods and workers are without economic value unless a demand exists. The result, as Fromm sees it, is that modern man, "transformed into a commodity, experiences his life forces as an investment which must bring him the maximum profit obtainable under existing market conditions."[26] His innate diversity harnessed, man becomes an "alienated automaton" —suggestive, says Wiener, of the Leibnitzian automata—and if his particular abilities are not in demand or if a surplus of these abilities exists, he is discarded by the system. Such a process is not only "a degradation of man's very nature," Wiener maintains, but "economically a waste of the great human values which man possesses."[27]

The Crying of Lot-49 (1966), Pynchon's second novel,

deals with entropy as it relates to communications and with the waste of human values in a mechanistic society. At one point in the novel, Oedipa Maas, the protagonist, reflects upon the vast numbers of Americans who have been discarded by the social machine. "She had heard all about excluded middles; they were bad shit, to be avoided; but how had it ever happened here, with the chances once so good for diversity?"[28] The late Pierce Inverarity, of whose estate Oedipa is executor, represents one answer to this question. Not only does he own an entire city, San Narciso, but every commercial enterprise Oedipa encounters in her attempts to trace the origin of the mysterious Tristero organization, an underground mail delivery service, from munitions plants (Yoyodyne) to cigarette manufacturers to used book stores, are either owned or controlled by Inverarity. Such uneven distribution of wealth results in "futureless" human beings, like those pitifully poor who trade cars with Oedipa's husband, Mucho Maas:

> ... Negro, Mexican, cracker, a parade seven days a week, bringing the most godawful of trade-ins: motorized, metal extensions of themselves, of their families and what their whole lives must be like ... , inside smelling hopelessly of children, supermarket booze, two, sometimes three generations of cigarette smokers, or only of dust—and when the cars were swept out you had to look at the actual residue of these lives ... , all the bits and pieces coated uniformly, like a salad of despair, in a gray dressing of ash, condensed exhaust, dust, body wastes.... (13-14)

Even those employed by Inverarity lack freedom. Stanley Koteks, an engineer at Yoyodyne, tells Oedipa that in the name of "teamwork" all engineers must sign away patent rights to any inventions made while employed by the corporation. "Nobody wanted them to invent—only perform their little role in a design ritual, already set down for them in some procedures handbook" (88). In every case, Oedipa discovers, the mass of men fall victim to the social machine, either discarded as waste or reduced to the role of functionary. Oedipa herself, long before the death of Inverarity, had intuitively perceived the walls of the prison-house. In Mexico City with Pierce, while viewing a Varo painting of a beautiful girl "magically" imprisoned in a tower, Oedipa realizes that she "had really never escaped the confinement of [her own] tower" (20). At this point Oedipa is unaware of exactly what she desires escape from. As she becomes further entangled in the mysteries of Tristero, however, Oedipa realizes that the imprisoning "magic, anonymous and malignant, visited on her from outside and for no reason at all" (21), is the same "magic" that incarcerates some in prisons of poverty and others in straitjackets of organizational "efficiency": our absurd modern mass society.

The Crying of Lot-49, then, like Heller's *Catch-22*, launches a protest against the powers of modern mass society. Pynchon's concern is less with mass society as such, however, than with the fact that man has allowed such circumstances to evolve in the first place. Man has become "conditioned . . . to accept any San Narciso among [the land's] most tender flesh without a reflex or a cry . . ." (181). He has allowed corporations to take credit for his creative energies, because such "teamwork," as Stanley Koteks maintains, "is a way to avoid responsibility. It's a symptom of the gutlessness of the whole society" (85). Oedipa realizes that she, too, shares this "gutlessness" when, after hearing merchant Winthrop Tremaine's plans to increase production of swastikas and Schutzstaffel uniforms, she drives away, offering not one word of reproach. "You're chicken, she told herself, snapping her seat belt. This is America, you live in it, you let it happen" (150).

Yet in the midst of all this passive acceptance Oedipa encounters "another world's intrusion into this one," what the professional revolutionary Jesus Arrabal calls "an anarchist miracle" (120). There exists, she learns, a secret organization of the "nameless" everywhere. All machines use energy, and the members of W.A.S.T.E. constitute the wasted energy of the American social machine. Engaged in revolution, their activities are neither treasonous nor perhaps even defiant (124) but entail "a calculated withdrawal from the life of the Republic, from its machinery."

> Whatever else was being denied them out of hate, indifference
> to the power of their vote, loopholes, simple ignorance, this
> withdrawal was their own, unpublicized, private. Since they
> could not have withdrawn into a vacuum . . . , there had to
> exist the separate, silent, unsuspected world. (124-25).

They offer, Oedipa comes to realize, "a real alternative to
the exitlessness, to the absence of surprise to life, that har-
rows the head of everybody in America . . ." (170). Unlike
the disinherited citizens of Rosewater, Indiana, in Vonnegut's *God Bless You, Mr. Rosewater*, the disinherited of
Pynchon's novel refuse to become resigned to their state.

The name of their organization is an acronym formed
from the initial letters of their motto: "We Await Silent
Tristero's Empire." As the motto indicates, their tactics
consist of "aloofness" and "waiting," but "waiting above
all; if not for another set of possibilities . . . , then at least,
at the very least, . . . for a symmetry of choices to break
down, to go skew" (181). At the moment this "symmetry
of choices" crumbles, Tristero's empire will have arrived.
To the Scurvhamite Puritans of the seventeenth century,
part of the universe "ran off" a principle opposite to God,
"something blind, soulless; a brute automatism that led to
eternal death" (155). This "automatism" was symbolized
by Tristero. In 1964, present time in the novel, Tristero no
longer represents a principle of annihilation in a Manichean
universe, but—updated by W.A.S.T.E.—it stands for the entropic process itself.

Nowhere is this explicitly stated in the novel. But that
Pynchon has entropy in mind is suggested in a scene that at
first reading seems unrelated to the rest of the novel. While
in Berkeley, Oedipa visits John Nefastis, sexual deviant and
television addict, who is experimenting with a Maxwell's
Demon. Maxwell's Demon is part of a theory offered in
1871 by Scotch physicist Clerk Maxwell. Maxwell visualized
a gas-filled box divided into two compartments connected
by a door. At this door sits a tiny demon who allows the
passage of only high velocity molecules into one compart-
ment and only low velocity molecules into the other. The
temperature difference could then be used to produce

work. Thermal energy can be transformed into mechanical energy only if there is a difference in temperature between two parts of the system. The transformation of thermal into mechanical energy, however, always diminishes the temperature differences, hence diminishing the potential for further work. By "sorting" hot and cold molecules, Maxwell's demon could prevent this entropic loss of heat, and perpetual motion would result.[29]

The fallacy in Maxwell's theory is that there is no way the demon can "see" which molecules are which. To prevent the increase of entropy, any light particles in the box must exist in equilibrium with the gas molecules, and such uniformity of radiation leaves the demon as "blind" as if there were no light present at all. In order for the demon to derive the information necessary to separate the hot from the cold molecules, light from another source must be provided, yet such an addition would also destroy the equilibrium between light particles and gas molecules in the box. This would lead to an increase in entropy, canceling out any local entropy decrease achieved by the demon's efforts. The problem, in other words, is one of communication. Could the proper information be obtained by the demon without the use of outside light, entropy would indeed be prevented.

Nefastis' idea is that a human being, a "sensitive," can communicate "at some deep psychic level" with the demon. The demon "passes his data on to the sensitive, and the sensitive must reply in kind" (105). By keeping their energies cycling, the "sensitive" and the demon prevent any loss of energy, thus violating the second law of thermodynamics. "Communication," says Nefastis, "is the key" (105).

Communication also holds the key to the success of W.A.S.T.E. While "reserving their lies, recitations of routine, arid betrayals of spiritual poverty, for the official government delivery system," the members of W.A.S.T.E. are "truly communicating" via their own secret delivery system (170). Since successful communication is an anti-entropic process, the members of W.A.S.T.E. form pockets of organization in a slowly decaying social system. When capitalistic society finally goes the way of all closed systems, the disinherited forming the membership of W.A.S.T.E. will emerge, reclaiming at last their lost inheritance: America and the possibilities it originally offered.

Pynchon never reveals whether the Tristero system is a reality, a hoax, or a hallucination (170-71). Like her namesake, Oedipa has pursued the mystery with increasing apprehension. At the novel's end she awaits the crying of Lot-49, the auctioning-off of a group of stamps bearing the sign of Tristero, a muted postal horn. By contacting whoever buys the lot, Oedipa hopes to discover the truth behind the mystery of Tristero. On this note of hope the novel concludes, a note that distinguishes the novel from those of Kurt Vonnegut, Jr., who portrays similar situations but offers little chance for change.

Pynchon's novel, in fact, is like *Catch-22* in that it is finally a radical protest novel. Built into the structure of the novel is an alternative to the present political and economic system in America. What Pynchon would substitute seems to be the idealized anarchy Jesus Arrabal dreams of, in which "the soul's talent for consensus allows the masses to work together without effort, automatic as the body itself" (120). In the ballroom scene of Chapter Five, Pynchon offers a comic version of what his Utopia would be like. Oedipa watches as delegates to a convention of deaf mutes dance, then is asked to join in:

> Each couple on the floor danced whatever was in the fellow's head: tango, two-step, bossa nova, slop. . . . There would have to be collisions. The only alternative was some unthinkable order of music, many rhythms, all keys at once, a choreography in which each couple meshed easy, predestined. Something they all heard with an extra sense atrophied in herself. She followed her partner's lead, . . . waiting for the collisions to begin. But none came. . . . Jesus Arrabal would have called it an anarchist miracle. (131-32)

Pynchon seems to desire a radical freedom, an anarchist ball where one dances to his own rhythms, not to the ritualized beat of mass society. While his alternative sounds as simplistic as "do your own thing" and probably risks chaos, the present system, Pynchon would argue, guarantees chaos.

Neither Pynchon's radical political inclinations nor his scientific erudition, however, account for his novelistic achievements. Rather it is the considerable skill with which he weaves these and other materials into the complex fabric of his art. Science, particularly the principle of entropy, is the complex figure in the carpet which gives unity to both *V.* and *The Crying of Lot-49*. Though the absurdist vision wavers somewhat in both novels, particularly the latter, which seems to protest absurdity rather than present it, each represents an impressive accomplishment. Thomas Pynchon must rank among the more talented younger novelists writing in America today.

V

Paradigms of Absurdity:
The Absurdist Novels of John Barth

THE PUBLICATION of John Barth's *The Sot-Weed Factor* in 1960 launched an avalanche of admiration, outrage and confusion, but mostly confusion. Most critics found it difficult to "place" the novel in any of the traditional slots. Richard Kostelanetz, for example, tried fitting it into "the American tradition of anti-realistic romance, particularly those novels concerned with individual man and oppressive civilization . . . ."[1] Earl Rovit, on the other hand, called the novel a "shallow parody." "For a twentieth-century writer to present an 800-page novel while denying himself access to the speech of his own time," complained Rovit, referring to Barth's decision to write *The Sot-Weed Factor* entirely in the idiom of the seventeenth century, "is to suggest that parody has become that kind of imitation which is frozen into the inflexible forms of that which it is meant to ridicule or use as a means of ridicule."[2] Others commenting on the novel included *Time*, which read it as a "genuinely serious comedy," Edmund Fuller, who called it a "ludicrous mock-heroic adventure," and Russel H. Miller, who declared that although the novel's philosophy might be modern, its form is that of a traditional mock-epic.[3] Another critic saw *The Sot-Weed Factor* as an "historical novel,"[4] still another as an "anti-historical novel,"[5] and yet a third as a "mock historical novel."[6] From the midst of this confusion one generally shared question seemed to emerge. Robert Garvis, writing in *Commentary*, used that question as the title of his long, disparaging review, "What Happened to John Barth?"[7]

The question has relevance. Before *The Sot-Weed Factor*, Barth's reputation as a writer of conventional, if distinctive, novels seemed secure. In fact, his first novel, *The Floating Opera*, was runner-up for the National Book Award in 1956. When Barth's second novel, *The End of the Road*, appeared in 1958 displaying the same traditional character-istics as the first, it seemed Barth would remain content working within existing novelistic conventions. *The Sot-Weed Factor*, however, quickly ended such speculations. In length alone, Barth's leviathan of a novel exceeds by two-hundred pages the combined length of his two previous novels. Not only does Barth discard realism in the novel, but he flaunts artificiality. Characterized by an elaborately structured plot, the novel includes a proliferation of out-rageous coincidences, a host of caricatures and "stock" comic-figures, irrelevant digressions, and a style that is or-nate and purposely exaggerated. When Barth followed *The Sot-Weed Factor* in 1966 with *Giles Goat-Boy*, which is just as baroque and almost as long, it became clear that *The Sot-Weed Factor* represented more than a temporary quirk of Barth's imagination. Quite clearly, Barth intended to steer the novel in a new direction. But whether this was the direction of decadence and represented the last gasp of a dying genre or the direction of innovation and was in-tended to revitalize the novel, no one seemed sure.

According to Barth, both extremes—decadence and re-juvenation—contributed to these novels. Concerning deca-dence, Barth agrees, "with reservations and hedges," that "the novel, if not narrative literature generally, if not the printed word altogether, has by this hour of the world just about shot its bolt."[8] Yet, he maintains, novelists may con-tinue producing books during the "apocalyptic ambience." Their problem, of course, lies in choosing what kind of novel to write. On the one hand, they may choose as models what Barth calls "turn-of-the-century-type novels [written] in more or less mid-twentieth-century language

... about contemporary people and topics. ..."[9] These models should be avoided if possible, however. "Contemporary writers can't go on doing what's been done, and done better," Barth explains. "I revere Flaubert and Tolstoy, Hemingway and Faulkner; but they're finished as objects of interest to the writer. My God, we're living in the last third of the twentieth century. We can't write nineteenth-century novels."[10] In fact, such novels were brought to a "kind of conclusion," Barth maintains, by Joyce and Kafka.

Novelists who succeeded Joyce and Kafka, the most accomplished of whom—in Barth's opinion—are Beckett and Borges, provide the second model for contemporary novelists. Yet just as Joyce and Kafka "concluded" the particular form of the novel they developed, so have Beckett and Borges brought their version of the novel to another kind of conclusion. "From both," Barth explains, "I get ... an esthetic of silence. Beckett is moving toward silence, refining language out of existence, working toward the point where there's nothing more to say. And Borges writes as if literature had already been done and he's writing footnotes of imaginary texts."[11] The alternatives provided by modern novelistic models, then, seem to be "technically old-fashioned" forms, on the one hand, and simple silence, on the other.

Barth chooses a third alternative, however, one better suited to his "temperament." "The future of the novel is dubious," he admits. "OK. So I start with the premise of the 'end of literature' and try to turn it against itself. I go back to Cervantes, Fielding, Sterne, the 'Arabian Nights,' to the artificial frame and the long connected tales."[12] Such ironic imitation, Barth points out, is where the novel began, "with *Quixote* imitating *Amadis of Gaul*, Cervantes pretending to be the Cid Hamete Benegeli (and Alonso Quijano pretending to be Don Quixote), or Fielding parodying Richardson."[13] But by recasting these prototypic forms in new, farcial models, the writer achieves "something new," something that "*may be* quite serious and passionate despite its farcical aspect."[14]

This farcical imitation constitutes the primary difference between what Barth calls a "proper novel" and what he terms a "deliberate imitation of a novel, or a novel imitative of other sorts of documents." Whereas the first "has been historically inclined to attempt . . . to imitate actions more or less directly," the latter seeks "to represent not life directly but a representation of life." Consequently, the conventional devices of a proper novel—"cause and effect, linear anecdote, characterization, authorial selection, arrangement, and interpretation—[which] have long since been objected to as obsolete notions," remain available to the "imitative" novelists. Because "imitations-of-novels" are parodies of the "proper novel," all objections to the use of conventional devices are obviated. Moreover, "imitations-of-novels" such as *The Sot-Weed Factor* and *Giles Goat-Boy* are able to reject as obsolete the very devices they employ to effect this rejection. On a larger scale, such novels mock the novel as an outmoded genre while at the same time keeping the genre alive, infusing it, as it were, with original blood. Ironic and farcical imitation, then, allows the novelist paradoxically to turn what Barth calls a "felt ultimacy" of our time, the death of the novel, "into material and means for his work—*paradoxically* because by doing so he transcends what had appeared to be his refutation . . . ," a transcendence that results in "new and original literature."[15]

Much of the above has been discussed as "reflexive burlesque" in Chapter One and at various places throughout this study. The particular use Barth makes of reflexive burlesque needs further examination, because it serves as his most significant single device, one he uses in a multiplicity of ways. In a larger sense, the novel as burlesque becomes in Barth's hands an extended metaphor for his concerns. In short, his novels become paradigms of or metaphors for the absurdity he examines. Vonnegut's *The Sirens of Titan* and Pynchon's *V.* have already been discussed in similar terms. The first was examined as an extended metaphor for a purposeless universe; the second, as a metaphor for entropy and the quantum theory. Barth, however, applies yet another turn of the screw. Because his absurdist novels are imitations of conventionally structured novels, their reflection of absurdity becomes indirect. Essentially, they become inverted paradigms, ironic metaphors.

This use of the novel as paradigm can be best appreciated if the precise nature of Barth's absurdist vision is first understood. In both *The Sot-Weed Factor* and *Giles Goat-Boy*, Barth presents a world characterized by more disorder than continuity, by more incongruity than meaning. Henry Burlingame of *The Sot-Weed Factor* acknowledges this absurdity when he apprises Ebenezer Cooke, his former pupil and the novel's protagonist, of the true nature of the universe. "The world's indeed a flux . . . ," proclaims Burlingame; "the very universe is naught but change and motion."[16] So complex and absurd a universe cannot be reduced to any set of rational standards. Nor can man, as part of this protean reality, be accurately formulated. Indeed, reason becomes all but impotent to deal with the shifting, elusive reality of an absurd universe.

Barth's distrust of rational systems receives its most direct treatment in *The End of the Road*. At one point in that novel, Jacob Horner, the protagonist, says, "to turn experience into speech—that is, to classify, to categorize, to conceptualize, to grammarize, to syntactify it—is always a betrayal of experience, a falsification of it. . . ."[17] Horner refers here to the classification of experience, but in principle what he says applies to all "rational" formulations, which—in Barth's view—distort rather than explain reality. This distortion even extends to the application of linguistic labels. "Assigning names to things," Horner muses later in the novel, "is like assigning roles to people: it is necessarily a distortion . . . " (135).

Such simplification, Horner goes on to say, often proves necessary before reality "can be dealt with at all" (112). Those whom Barth calls "connoisseurs," however, realize such "precise falsification" represents no more than "adroit, careful myth-making" (113) and consider it "good clean fun" (135). "Connoisseurs" recognize all rational formulations for the necessary expedients they are—useful devices that only seem to isolate what is really continuous, to homogenize what is really different, and to make permanent what is constantly shifting. "Connoisseurs," that is, never confuse the formulation of reality for reality itself.

Neither Ebenezer Cooke, protagonist of *The Sot-Weed Factor*, nor George, protagonist of *Giles Goat-boy*, qualify as connoisseurs. Both attempt to order the world around artificial values, bogus conceptions of their own identities and of the nature of reality. Both soon discover that their ordering won't work. A fluid reality makes all intellectual footholds slippery. Chaos beats erratically at the heart of human existence and will not be harnessed.

At age thirty, Ebenezer Cooke chooses innocence as his value, thereafter viewing virginity as the "essence" of his selfhood. "What am I?" he declares. "*Virgin*, sir! *Poet*, sir! I am a virgin and a poet; less than mortal and more: not a man, but mankind! I shall regard my innocence as badge of my strength and proof of my calling: let her who's worthy of't take it from me" (60). Before making this "existential" decision, Cooke had suffered from the same disease Barth calls "cosmopsis" in *The End of the Road*. The multiple possibilities of a fluctuating universe paralyze Eben's will. He simply cannot choose a mode of action. Ironically, this affliction had "protected" Eben's virginity through the years. Though often presented with the opportunity for sexual engagement, Eben "could never choose one role to play over all the rest he knew, and so always ended up either turning down the chance or, what was more usually the case, retreating gracefully and in confusion, if not always embarrassment" (45). The correlation between Eben's past vacillations and his present virtue casts discredit upon the poet's belief that his physical innocence symbolizes spiritual purity.

Despite the apparent falsity of his chosen role, Eben charges into the world of experience bearing innocence as his standard, only to discover his values inadequate to cope with life's complexity. Though prepared to accept Lord Baltimore as the epitome of good and John Coode as the apotheosis of evil, Eben soon becomes confused as to their aims and even about their correct identities. Similarly, he elevates justice to a transcendent level, "noumenal and pure." But the New World's brand of justice—blindfold off and hand out—in no way relates to Eben's ideals. When he rises to champion justice in a Maryland court, he succeeds only in losing his estate to an agent working to corrupt the colonies.

As Eben encounters shock after cruel shock, the scales of innocence drop gradually from his eyes, until the falseness of his stance becomes evident even to him. "When erst I entered the lists of Life," he admits late in the novel, "Virginity was a silken standard that I waved, all bright and newly stitched. 'Tis weatherblast and run now, and so rent by the shocks of combat e'en its bearer might mistake it for a boot rag" (629). Willingly, Eben puts aside the tattered banner, convinced that his innocence had exceeded mere folly, shading finally into sin, for others besides himself had suffered the consequences of his ignorance. "That is the crime I stand indicted for," he says, " . . . the crime of innocence, whereof the Knowledger must bear the burthen. There's the true Original Sin our souls are born in: not that Adam learned, but that he *had* to learn—in short, that he was innocent" (739).

When Eben consummates his marriage to Joan Toast, he expiates his sin of innocence by symbolically losing it. More importantly, since Joan Toast—pox-ridden, dope-addicted prostitute—stands as the "very sign and emblem" (468) of the world, Eben freely embraces a world stripped of all illusions and ideals. His painful discovery that neither man nor the world can be made to fit any abstract or rational formula, that one must accept "what is the case" without embellishment or hope for understanding it, fulfills Henry Burlingame's definition of "man's lot":

> He is by mindless lust engendered and by mindless wrench expelled, from the Eden of the womb to the motley, mindless world. He is Chance's fool, the toy of aimless Nature—a mayfly flitting down the winds of Chaos!

... "Here we sit upon a blind rock hurtling through a vacuum, racing to the grave." 'Tis our fate to search, Eben, and do we seek our souls, what we find is a piece of that same black Cosmos whence we sprang and through which we fall: the infinite wind of space.... (344-45)

Burlingame, who functions as Eben's foil in the novel, represents the only viable stance for man in an absurd world. Whereas Ebenezer seeks a permanence somewhere above the random flux of human events, Henry submerses himself, as Richard W. Nolland points out, in the "shifting and ambiguous historical process."[18] Whereas Ebenezer, in asserting his "identity," embraces what he understands as being; Henry, in searching for his rightful parentage, remains satisfied with becoming. Eben requires an absolute to shield himself from reality; Henry, on the other hand, is "a glutton for the great world, of which [he] ne'er can see and learn enough" (145). Burlingame carries this "cosmophilism" to such extremes, in fact, that he literally makes love to the world (328, 497). Moreover, as Tony Tanner suggests, Burlingame's numerous identities reflect Barth's belief that life is a never-ending series of roles.[19] In an absurd universe, identity becomes tenuous; essential selfhood, impossible.[20] Finally, that Burlingame's understanding of the true nature of reality exceeds Ebenezer's becomes apparent early in the novel. After a lengthy debate between Eben and Henry concerning selfhood, Ebenezer remarks: "Marry, your discourse hath robbed me of similes: I know naught immutable and sure!" To which Burlingame wisely replies: " 'Tis the first step on the road to Heaven" (128).

Just as Ebenezer must learn the wisdom of Burlingame's counsel experientially, so in *Giles Goat-Boy* must George learn the nature of reality by confronting it. Like Cooke, George chooses rather than discovers his identity. "I'm going to be a hero," he announces to Max Spielman, his tutor and keeper, without really understanding what a hero is. As the novel progresses, he comes to realize that the traditional conception of the hero no longer has relevance.

George, who "gimps" along Oedipus-like because of a "birth defect" acquired when the computer that sired him also crippled him, discovers that although—like Oedipus—he may achieve a certain measure of understanding, he cannot pass that understanding on to his society. Unlike the heroes of old, he cannot help his society in any way at all, for—given the nature of an absurd reality—any "philosophies of life" he might recommend would falsify reality by oversimplifying its complexities and would result, as he painfully discovers, in more harm than good.

Before assuming his heroic "identity," George had intuitively comprehended something of the true nature of reality. Reflecting upon the "Facts of [his] own existence and nature," George sensed the shifting nature of human existence and the artificiality of all formulations of that existence:

> There was no birthdate, birthplace, or ancestry to define me. I had seen generations of kids grow to goathood, reproduce themselves, and die, like successive casts of characters. . . . I had lived in goatdom as Billy Bocksfuss the Kid, now I meant to live in studentdom as George the Undergraduate; surely there would be other roles in other realms, an endless succession of names and natures. Little wonder I looked upon my life and the lives of others as a kind of theatrical impromptu, self-knowledge as a kind of improvisation, and moral injunctions, such as those of the *Fables*, whether high-minded or wicked, as so many stage directions. (81)

Eben, too, had been nearer an understanding of the human condition when, at age twelve or thirteen, he composed his first poem:

> Figures so strange, no God design'd
> To be a Part of Human-kind,
> But wanton Nature, void of Rest,
> Moulded the brittle Clay in Jest. (124)

George, like Eben, forgets his early perceptions and attempts to order reality around a personal set of values. Fancying himself a Messiah or Grand Tutor, George takes his first Tutorial position while debating Maurice Stoker, who has devoted his life in true "Dean O' Flunks" fashion to the perpetration of disorder. The "first reality of life on campus," says George, "must be the clear distinction between Passage and Failure, the former of which was always and only passed, the latter flunked" (420). As Robert Scholes points put in his comprehensive analysis of the novel, George's fundamentalist stance originates as a mere debating ploy, "more in hopes of unsettling [his] adversary than of instructing either [Stoker] or [himself]" (420).[21] Yet just as Eben had converted the chance circumstance of his virginity into an ideal, so does George seize upon his chance rhetoric as truth, not only believing it himself but disseminating it as the new gospel. Indeed, the only difference between George's stance and the several taken by Harold Bray, multi-faced anti-Tutor and master of empty rhetoric, is that George sincerely believes his sophistry.[22]

When pandemonium threatens West Campus as the result of George's ministry (532-35), he reverses his righteousness, declaring that "Failure is passage" (552). Adopting his new dogma, George denies as false all categories, all divisions, even sexual ones; "for what were *male* and *female*," he reasons, "if not the most invidious of the false polarities into which undergraduate reason was wont to sunder Truth?" (638). His second conception of the nature of things proves as disastrous as the first, however. His decree that the "flunked" are "passed" unleashes anarchy: The cold riot grows hot, the dangerously insane are freed from institutions, workers neglect their duties, and moral standards are discarded. "Once more," the goat-boy realizes, "I'd been all wrong, in what wise I was too miserable to care" (641).

George's error, as he comes to realize, lay in his belief that the world or man's response to it can be formulated in the first place. As the University crumbles into chaos, George struggles for understanding, the "paradoxes" of his second tutorial position becoming "paroxysms" in the effort. "Passage *was* Failure," he strains to reason, "and Failure Passage; yet Passage was Passage, Failure Failure! Equally true, none was the Answer; the two were not different, neither were they the same; and *true* and *false*, and *same* and *different*—Unspeakable! Unnamable! Unimaginable! Surely my mind must crack!" (650). At that moment, Stoker shouts a warning to two prisoners: "Don't try to get loose!" Since Stoker represents the principle of perversity and contrariness, George, who hears Stoker's cry, instinctively does the opposite, immediately "letting go," whereupon "relief went through [him] like a purge"—

> And as if in signal of my freedom, over the reaches of the campus the bell of Tower Clock suddenly rang out . . . . As I listened astonished, the strokes mounted—*one, two, three, four* —each bringing from my pressed eyes the only tears they'd spilled since a fateful late-June morn many terms past, out in the barns. *Sol, la, ti*, each a tone higher than its predecessor, unbinding, releasing me—then *do*: my eyes were opened; I was delivered. (650-51)

As Robert Scholes points out, "the last note, musically the octave-completing *do*, stands also for the simple imperative urging action: do!"[23] One earns salvation, if at all, by active participation in life. Understanding comes experientially only. Like Burlingame, one must thrust himself into the midst of life, discarding all formulas, casting concepts and systems aside, content always with becoming, never to fully be. As George had earlier realized in a rare burst of perception, "Nothing . . . was simply *the case* forever and aye, only '*this* case' " (81). All positivistic conceptions of existence disregard more reality than they account for.

The nature of George's final illumination can be better understood if seen in terms of Joseph Campbell's *The Hero With a Thousand Faces*. In an interview, Barth admitted the influence on *Giles Goat-Boy* of Campbell's fascinating study of the wandering hero in myth and literature. After having it pointed out to him that Ebenezer Cooke qualified on twenty-three of Lord Raglan's twenty-five prerequisites for the ritual hero, Barth's interest was aroused. "I got excited over Raglan and Joseph Campbell," he says, "who may be a crank for all I know or care, and I really haven't been able to get that business off my mind—the tradition of the wandering hero. The only way I could use it would be to make it comic, and there will be some of that in *Giles Goat-Boy*."[24]   A comparison of Barth's novel with Campbell's analysis indicates how liberally Barth did borrow from the tradition of the hero. Indeed, most of the requisites Campbell cites occur in *Giles Goat-Boy*.

The "first stage of the mythological journey," Campbell designates as "The Call to Adventure." It "signifies that destiny has summoned the hero and transferred his spiritual center of gravity from within the pale of his society to a zone unknown."[25]   George's "call" occurs when he discovers while still at the Ag Hill Goat Farm that he is not a goat at all, but a man. The unknown zone to which he must travel not only includes the world of West Campus, but the world of human existence as well. "I want to be a man," he declares, signaling the start of his adventure. "The goats still struck me as far superior in almost every respect to the humans I'd seen and heard of: stronger, calmer, nobler; more handsome, more loving, more reliable. But the humans, for better or worse, were vastly more interesting . . ." (24-25).

Often accompanying the hero on his journey is "a protective figure (often a little old crone or old man) who provides the adventurer with amulets against the dragon forces he is about to pass."[26]   Functioning in this role is Max Spielman, the old scientist who, Virgil-like, conducts George as far as reason can before yielding to Anastasia, the Beatrice-figure, at the novel's equivalent of what Campbell calls "the threshold of Paradise,"[27]   an occurrence to be discussed in detail later. As Stoker notices (191), the amulet George carries consists of the testicles of Tommy Redfearn, the goat George killed out of jealousy earlier in the novel.

The various adventures George encounters on the road to his ultimate revelation constitute his "Road of Trials." In passing the "Trial by Turnstile" at Scrape-goat Grate, which allows George to enter West Campus and confer with its Chancellor, Lucky Rexford, he fulfills the traditional step in the heroic journey Campbell calls "The Crossing of the

First Threshold," which lies "at the entrance to the zone of magnified power."[28]   When he descends with the Satan-like Stoker into the chaotic, Pit-like Furnace Room, "where great fires seemed to rage beneath the floor" (177), George reenacts the traditional "voyage to the underworld."[29] When he passes three times through WESCAC's belly, he reenacts the traditional passage through the belly of the whale.[30]   The mythic hero gained release from the whale's belly by generating a fire with "fire sticks" that kills the monster. This act, Campbell indicates, "is symbolic of the sex act. . . . The hero making fire in the whale is a variant of the sacred marriage,"[31]   that marriage which will bring about the hero's illumination. During George's final descent into WESCAC's belly, he copulates with Anastasia, a comic variant on the traditional myth, short circuits the monstrous computer, and gains release from his philosophical confusion. Coupled with Anastasia in the darkness of WESCAC's belly, his head covered by his mother's purse, George discovers "the University whole and clear." Oedipus-like, he sees "in the darkness blinding light! The end of the University! Commencement Day!" (673).

George's illumination offers interesting parallels to Campbell's discussion of the traditional hero's moment of vision. According to a variety of ancient myths, God—who is both male and female—originally created man in His own vision, that is, "created him androgynous"—

> The removal of the feminine into another form symbolizes the beginning of the fall from perfection into duality; and it was naturally followed by the discovery of the duality of good and evil, exile from the garden where God walks on earth, and thereupon the building of the wall of Paradise, constituted on the "coincidences of opposites," by which Man (now man and woman) is cut off from not only the vision but even the recollection of the images of God.[32]

At the moment of his illumination, the hero—who has contained "the godly powers sought" within his own heart all the time[33] —recollects the "divine form" of God and regains wisdom.[34]   He comes to understand the secret of

"The Cosmogonic Cycle," that all things exist as part of a single creation, are the One become the many, yet remain the One undivided. "The great deed of the supreme hero is to come to the knowledge of this unity in multiplicity . . . ."[35]

When George enters WESCAC the last time, he enters "as one" with Anastasia. When asked the first of WESCAC's questions designed to identify the true Grand Tutor, George and Anastasia "rose up joined, found the box, and joyously pushed the buttons, both together, holding them fast as [they] held each other" (672). By this action, they acknowledge the truth of the androgynity of humanity as it was at the beginning of the "Cosmognic Cycle" and as it will again be when the cycle is complete. Immediately, George receives the sacred knowledge of unity existing in multiplicity:

> In the sweet place that contained me there was no East, no West, but an entire, single, seamless campus: Turnstile, Scrape-goat Grate, the Mall, the barns, the awful fires of the Power-house, the balmy heights of Founder's Hill—I saw them all; rank jungles of Frumentius, Nikolay's cold fastness, teeming T'any—all one, and one with me. *Here* lay with *there*, *tick* clipped *tock*, *all* serviced *nothing*; I and My Ladyship, all, were one. (731)

Having gained an understanding of the novel's equivalent of "The Cosmognic Cycle," The Cyclological Hypothesis or Spielman's Law, "as perhaps Max could never" (675); George kisses its sign, Anastasia's Mount of Venus, the fount and symbol of all creation.[36]

George's union with Anastasia parallels the mythic hero's marriage to the Queen Goddess. As Campbell explains, "Woman, in the picture language of mythology, represents the totality of what can be known. . . . The mystical marriage with the queen goddess of the world represents the hero's total mastery of life."[37] WESCAC, on the other hand, represents the ritualistic role of the hero's father, "through whom the young being passes on into the larger world."[38] Until his moment of illumination, the hero traditionally views the father as an ogre, for the father stands as "the sign of the future task" the hero must perform before insight is acquired. He represents, that is, the road of trials the hero must endure before experiencing his ultimate vision. After illumination, however, the hero realizes "that father and mother reflect each other, and are in essence the same."[39] George, too, had thought WESCAC a "Troll" because "it stood between Failure and Passage" (676). After his vision, however, he comes to realize that WESCAC "partook of both" passage and failure, "served both, and was in itself true emblem of neither. . . . Black cap and gown of naked Truth, it screened from the general eye what only the few, Truth's lovers and tutees, might look on bare and not be blinded" (676).

Barth does not offer this mystical concept of a "seamless," all-in-One, One-in-all universe seriously. Like *The Sot-Weed Factor*, *Giles Goat-Boy* is an imitative farce, one that mocks the idea of the hero as an obsolete notion belonging to a less complicated time when beliefs in man's noble stature still persisted. "I'm interested in the myth of the hero," Barth has said, referring to *Giles Goat-Boy*. "The trick was to be fully conscious of it—to satirize it, to parody it—but with compassion. . . ."[40] Aside from parody, however, George's vision serves as a kind of ironic metaphor for Barth's absurd universe. The goat-boy's insight into the vast and limitless nature of things extends beyond his powers to communicate that vision; it exceeds the bounds of formulation. "How to speak the unspeakable?" says George, identifying his dilemma (674). As a hero and authentic Grand Tutor, he must remain *incommunicado* forever, unable to take the traditional final step of the hero and return to his community "with his life-transmuting trophy."[41] George finds impossible what all heroes find difficult: "How render back into light-world language the speech-defying pronouncements of the dark? How communicate to people who insist on the exclusive evidence of their senses"—people such as Eblis Eierkopf, the multilensed scientist who insists he will believe a miracle only if he sees one—"the message of the all-generating void?"[42]

In the melancholy "Posttape," an older George, now thirty-three-and-a-third, speaks resignedly of his inability to express the inexpressible, "to teach the unteachable" (707). Nonetheless, an organized religion has sprung up, based not upon George's experience, but upon the interpretations of that experience by the "disciples" of Gilesianism, disciples who pervert the meaning of what George had learned in WESCAC's belly. I "know nothing of Gilesianism, New Curriculum, or Revised New Syllabus," George, now Giles, muses ironically—"but see termless Truth ..." (706). George's vision, then, symbolizes Barth's conception of a fluid reality that will not be systematized, that oozes incessantly through the formulating fingers of positivism, whether philosophical or scientific.

Seen in this light, the world of concepts and formulas— the world, in short, in which we live—becomes essentially artificial, a created world. The "world is our dream, our idea," writes Barth, "in which 'tenuous and eternal crevices of unreason' can be found to remind us that our creation is false, or at least fictive."[43] Barth reflects this fictive world in the exaggerated artificiality of his novels. "A different way to come to terms with the discrepancy between art and the Real Thing," Barth has said in a statement already quoted, "is to affirm the artificial element in art (you can't get rid of it anyway), and make the artifice part of your point ...."[44] The more obviously artificial Barth's novels are, the more paradigmatic they become of the fictive world he is treating, or at least of the fictive world represented in the art form he imitates. Thus, in a very real sense, the medium becomes the message.

Barth emphasizes the artifice of his novels in a number of ways. The various facets of his elaborate use of allegory in *Giles Goat-Boy* have been widely commented upon and need not be gone into here.[45] Suffice it to say that allegory, devoid of flesh and blood characters who have been replaced by two-dimensional representations of abstract notions or historical and literary figures, does not camouflage its artifice with realistic devices. Barth compounds an already artificial mode by adding a number of stock comic figures. Peter Greene, for example, appears as the stereotyped American WASP, complete with Puritan ethic and super-patriotism. Similarly, Eblis Eierkopf, who resembles Vonnegut's Felix Hoenikker, represents the stereotyped empiricist. In *The Sot-Weed Factor*, Barth—as he points out—also finds himself "using stock figures, stereotype Jews and Negroes, just for fun, as they did in the eighteenth century —blackamoors and village Jews and so forth."[46] To these obvious artifices, Barth adds a series of bizarre and fantastic incidents related in language purposely stilted and ornate. Moreover, since neither *Giles Goat-Boy* nor *The Sot-Weed Factor* is a "proper" novel, but "imitations-of-novels," they do not offer representations of reality at all but representations of representations of reality, removing them at least twice from the world of "objective reality" and further emphasizing their artificiality in the process. Thus Barth uses artificiality to expose artificiality. By presenting a farcical and exaggerated version of the world, not as the world is, but as it is erroneously conceived to be, Barth mocks the false conception and suggests cosmic absurdity by inversion.

His use of plot and structure affords Barth another means for reflecting absurdity ironically. This becomes especially evident in *The Sot-Weed Factor*. In writing that novel, Barth imitated the eighteenth-century novel generally but seems to have had *Tom Jones* particularly in mind. One of his intentions, he has said, "was to see if I couldn't make up a plot that was fancier than *Tom Jones. Tom Jones* is one of those novels that you don't want to end; you wish it could just keep going on and on. ... I like a flabbergasting plot. Nowadays, of course, you couldn't do it straight; it would have to be a formal farce."[47] As "formal farce," *The Sot-Weed Factor* not only parodies the eighteenth-century novel, but it mocks the world-view represented in the eighteenth-century novel.

The eighteenth-century mind envisioned a world of cosmic and social order, each reflecting the other. "The whole of living creation," writes Samuel Holt Monk, "was conceived to be carefully ordered and subtly graded in one vast 'chain of being,' descending from God, through an almost infinite number of pure intelligences, to man, and thence through the lower animals to microscopic forms of life, which finally end up in nothing."[48] Belief in this ordered universe prompted such confident assertions as Pope's "Whatever is is Right!" According to the aesthetic theory of the time, art should be, in Martin C. Battestin's terms, "fundamentally mimetic of this universal design."[49] An especially evident example of the mimetic theory as embodied in novel form, continues Battestin, is *Tom Jones*, which serves as a "paradigm of the Augustan world view," its design mirroring "a similar Order, a similar harmony and symmetry of parts, in Fielding's universe."[50]

Barth reflects this view of an ordered universe ironically in *The Sot-Weed Factor*. Like *Tom Jones*, it possesses a highly structured plot, one carefully conceived.[51] Since *The Sot-Weed Factor* is a "formal farce," the order reflected in its highly structured plot becomes an object of parody rather than affirmation. The novel turns back upon itself, rejecting the very order reflected in its form. By pushing the novel's "harmony of parts" into the realm of farcical exaggeration, Barth suggests disorder by inversion. Moreover, since the novel's theme clearly concerns absurdity, an incongruity exists between the novel's form and its philosophy. Like the ironic structure, however, this incongruity becomes functional, serving to reflect that incongruity which is part of an absurd universe.

Not merely the structure of *The Sot-Weed Factor*, but the incidents in the novel help to ironically reinforce Barth's absurdist vision. Most pertinent of these are the various coincidences that fill the novel. Any imitation of the eighteenth-century novel would of course include coincidences, that most salient of the genre's characteristics. Yet Barth transcends mere mimesis. In his hands, coincidence becomes a kind of metaphor in itself for absurdity, a significantly new device in the "new and original literature" Barth is creating.

In most eighteenth-century novels, coincidence functioned to suggest Providential design.[52] Nothing occurred by mere chance in an ordered universe. In Pope's famous phrase, "All Chance" was but "Direction, which thou canst not see," a part of the deity's ordered and omniscient government of his creation. As Wayne Booth points out, the narrator in *Tom Jones* functions as a kind of surrogate deity in the world of the novel.[53] The various coincidences that move the novel toward its comic conclusion reflect the narrator-author who orders these events, just as events of the real world signify the providential care of the deity who directs man toward some happy denouement.

Like *Tom Jones*, *The Sot-Weed Factor* progresses through a series of improbabilities to a fortunate conclusion. Ebenezer's chance meeting with Joan Toast shortly after he reaches Maryland is but one instance of the important role coincidence plays in the novel. At the novel's conclusion, all conflicts are resolved happily: Ebenezer consummates his marriage to Joan Toast, is reunited with Anna, regains his estate, and is awarded the Laureateship; Burlingame discovers his identity and prevents a war with the Indians. But this fortunate conclusion and the coincidences leading to it do not reflect providential design, as they would in a novel like *Tom Jones*, but mock the concept of providence, convert it into farce. Just as the structure of Barth's novel rejects the view of an ordered universe that it reflects, so do the coincidences in the novel reject the idea of design they embody. Once again, Barth employs the "imitation of a novel" not only to parody the kind of novel imitated but to mock the view of life represented in that novel. Through farce, Barth ironically suggests the absurdity that constitutes his main theme.

The use of coincidences suggests absurdity in yet another way. As indicated in the discussion of *Catch-22*, unexpected and improbable events serve as useful devices to indicate the lack of logic and predictability in an absurd universe. "Reality," says Barth, "is more preposterous than realism—wilder and less plausible."[54] Given such circumstances, the so-called improbable is as likely to occur as not. In an ordered universe, coincidences may be viewed as part of a benevolent Creator's cosmic plan. In a universe devoid of design or direction, however, they symbolize the sheer gratuitousness of human events.[55]

Other kinds of incidents Barth uses to reinforce his themes include those that emphasize man's animal nature. Human sexual as well as excremental activities receive graphic treatment. Like Swift, Barth discredits man's rational side by exaggerating his physical and instinctive as well as his emotional nature. While man often likes to consider himself rational, he becomes animalistic, as John C. Stubbs says of Todd Andrews, protagonist of *The Floating Opera*, "to the extent he is confronted by his emotions rather than his rational faculties."[56] Ebenezer, for example, maintains his virtue more by accident than personal design. He is often overpowered by lust, as when he attempts to "swive" Joan Toast as she hangs caught in the rigging of the Cyprian, only to be called away by Tom Pound, the pirate leader.

When man denies his animal side to emphasize the rational or "ideal," as Eben does in adopting the role of poet and virgin, he oversimplifies his complex humanity. Moreover, such a dichotomous attitude often severs his ties with other human beings. Todd Andrews, for example, bursts into laughter while in the act of coupling with Betty Jean Gunter because he sees himself in the mirror and recognizes the animalism of the sex act. A more serious episode occurs during the war when Todd meets an enemy soldier in a mudhole. Both men simultaneously feel fear (they both foul their britches), then love, as they begin to embrace and kiss. Later, while rationally reflecting upon his circumstances, Todd decides to kill the German, who still thinks of him as a friend and fellow sufferer.

Similarly, Ebenezer cannot enter into a completely meaningful relationship with either Anna or his wife until he puts aside his idealistic conceptions of the world. And George's vision occurs when he lies interlocked with Anastasia in sexual embrace. As Stubbs points out, only when man accepts the limits of his identity as "a complex, emotional, sexual animal," will he "be capable of feeling sympathy with other individuals who also live within the same limits."[57]   So Barth, like most other absurdist novelists, sees human commitment to other human beings—in short, love—as one of the few relative values available in an otherwise valueless universe.

McLuhanites and other prophets of doom have augured the death of the novel for some years now, until the possibility has become one of the "felt ultimacies" of our time. Acknowledging the possibility, Barth seizes it and transforms the ultimacy into materials and means for his concerns. The novels that result display remarkable vitality for products of a supposed "apocalyptic ambience." Moreover, by skillfully manipulating imitation and farce, Barth has woven language, incident, and form into an ironic metaphor for his absurdist vision, an inverted paradigm of his themes. More importantly, he has created a new and original literature from the alleged materials of decadence, insuring the life of the novel several more productive and useful years.

VI

Epilogue:
Camp, the Pop-Novel, and Absurdity

"AS CERTAINLY as the old God is dead," writes Leslie Fiedler in a recent essay, "so the old novel is dead."[1] To that cry a small but potent coterie of contemporary critics has recently rallied. The combined intelligence of this group cannot be denied. Norman Mailer, Susan Sontag, Norman Podhoretz, and Fiedler comprise its impressive nucleus. Except for Podhoretz, who would replace the "old" novel with journalism or at least with the so-called "non-fiction novels" of Truman Capote and the recent documentaries of Mailer, each of these critics has touched either directly or indirectly upon certain matters with which I have been concerned in previous chapters. Their arguments must therefore be answered before this study concludes.

Miss Sontag, perhaps the most stimulating of the "Novel is Dead" advocates, has recently challenged a concept long accepted as axiomatic by most critics: the indissolubility of form and content in the novel. Miss Sontag argues that novelists, and therefore critics, should ignore content or "meaning" altogether. Meaning, after all, is predicated on the belief that human experience can be ordered by the novelist's imagination. But "the discoveries of modern physics and of behavioral psychology have all but destroyed the old certainty of the human ordering of experience," as Louis D. Rubin, Jr., points out in his spirited defense of

121

the traditional novel, "so ... there can be no solid basis, whether in finite matter or human reason, upon which the novelist can erect his commentary."[2] Since the novel can no longer function in its traditional manner, Sontag suggests the novelist shift his emphasis from content to style and form. This would mean abandoning the "fancy that there really is such a thing as the content of a work of art," since that fancy forces attention away from artifice, which Sontag insists has an existence independent of content.[3] In fact, the old concept of content has become "a hindrance, a nuisance, a subtle or not so subtle philistinism."[4]

The new novel, as Sontag would have it, should exist solely as an art form, never as a testament. Only thus modified can it continue as a viable art form at all. "The novel as a form of art," Miss Sontag writes in her essay on Nathalie Sarraute, "has nothing to lose and everything to gain, by joining the revolution that has already swept over most of the other arts. It is time that the novel became what it is not, in England and America, with rare and unrelated exceptions: a form of art which people with serious and sophisticated taste in the other arts can take seriously."[5]

By Miss Sontag's own definition, technique without content becomes Camp. In fact, as Louis D. Rubin, Jr., correctly perceives, "at bottom" Miss Sontag proposes to replace the traditional novel with Camp.[6] Whereas the traditional novel attempted to discover meaning in human experience while it entertained, Camp seeks only to entertain. "The whole point of camp is to dethrone the serious."[7] Artifice, theatricality, become its ideals. Wholly aesthetic, "it incarnates a victory of 'style' over 'content,' 'aesthetics' over 'morality,' of irony over tragedy. ... Style is everything."[8]

According to Norman Mailer, the transition Sontag hopes for is well underway. Mailer divides the American novel of today into two categories: the novel of moral seriousness, the best example of which is *Herzog*, and Camp. *Herzog*, intrinsically dull in Mailer's opinion, succeeds only because we are desperate. "We were not ready to shoot Herzog. It all seemed too final if we did. Because then there would be nothing left but Camp. ..."[9] Camp, which emphasizes artifice at the expense of meaning, thereby destroys meaning. And the novel devoid of meaning ceases to be a novel in the traditional sense of the term.

Leslie Fiedler agrees with Sontag and Mailer that the traditional novel has ceased to exist as a viable genre. The forms of the novel most preferred by recent writers, he maintains, stand "at the farthest possible remove from art and avant-garde, the greatest distance from inwardness, analysis and pretension and, therefore, [are] immune to lyricism on the one hand and righteous social commentary on the other. It is not compromise by the market place they fear; on the contrary, they choose the genre most associated with exploitation by the mass media—notably, the Western, science fiction, and pornography."[10] The choice of such popular forms, Fiedler continues, stems from the awareness that when a medium of communication becomes obsolete, it must "become a form of entertainment, as recent developments in radio (the disappearance, for instance, of all high-minded commentators and pretentious playwrights) sufficiently indicate."[11] Thus the "truly new new novel" must acknowledge its own obsolescence, becoming a mode of entertainment and entertainment only, "anti-art as well as anti-serious."[12] The purpose in these novels of "parody or exaggeration or grotesque emulation of the classic past, as well as ... the adaptation and camping of pop forms,"[13] Fiedler maintains, functions simply to "close the gap ... between high culture and low, belles-lettres and pop art."[14] The use of exaggeration and burlesque is nothing more than a convenient and diverting way to dispose of the remains of an obsolete genre.

Fiedler and Sontag are correct in their observation that recent novelists have adapted pop and Camp forms. They err, however, in contending that the sole purpose of such presentation is to destroy all serious art. Both critics seem to have confused the form of recent novels—which is largely "non-serious"—with the intention of the novelists.

As I have tried to show in previous chapters, contemporary novelists of the absurd, despite their obvious humor, remain deadly serious. Their adaptation of pop and Camp forms provides them another method for rejecting the traditional concept of the novel. Historically, the novelist's aim has been to discover meaning in the universe or, at the very least, to give some shape to human life.[15] Indeed, as Morse Peckham has indicated, aestheticians and critics have traditionally assigned value to the novel precisely because "it offers us order."[16] By adapting Camp and pop forms, on the other hand, contemporary American novelists of the absurd repudiate the novel that presumes to "discover" order and significance in the universe. Their use of "non-serious" forms, then, is for serious ends. It allows them to expose the fraudulence of all narrative art that proclaims meaning where none exists.

Many recent examples of the adaptation of Camp and pop forms to absurdist novels in order to make a serious thematic statement are available. The often-cited episode in *The Sot-Weed Factor* when for seven pages two kitchen maids exchange various epithets for "whore" in two languages provides a good example of Camp. Taken out of context, the incident becomes a magnificent *tour de force*, an amusing diversion in no way related to the novel's theme. In context, however, the scene represents another example of Barth's special use of artifice to make his point. The very irrelevance of the scene—its very artificiality— makes it relevant to Barth's concern in the novel: the artificiality of a "rational" world. Thus Barth, like most contemporary absurdist novelists, uses Camp tactics, but for purposes antithetical to Camp as defined by Sontag.

This point can be further demonstrated by referring to Donald Barthelme's *Snow White* (1967). Barthelme's only novel to date, *Snow White* is an extended parody, an ingenious "put-on" that is perhaps the "purest" example of Camp yet published. Barthelme, however, does not emphasize artifice at the expense of meaning, as Sontag's definition of Camp would lead one to expect. On the contrary, *Snow White* demonstrates as few novels can the indissolubility of form and content in the novel. To be sure, the form of Barthelme's Camp masterpiece—the ways he manages and arranges character and incident and the use he makes of language—does obscure all coherent meaning or "content" in the novel, but this is precisely Barthelme's point. In writing a novel devoid of "meaning" in the traditional sense of that term, Barthelme denies the possibility of meaning in an absurd world. The form of his novel thus becomes an analogue to the absurd human condition.

At the end of Part I in *Snow White*, Barthelme offers a clue to the true nature of the novel. He inserts a series of fifteen questions designed to "test" the reader's comprehension. The questions begin seriously enough, suggesting that perhaps some meaning does exist in the novel. "Have you understood, in reading to this point," Barthelme asks, "that Paul is the prince-figure? . . . That Jane is the wicked step mother-figure?" Slowly, however, the questions become more absurd. Number ten—"Has the work, for you, a metaphysical dimension?"—seems reasonable enough, but is followed by: "What is it? (25 words or less)" After asking the reader to rate the work "on a scale of one to ten" while "holding in mind all works of fiction since the War, in all languages," Barthelme reveals that the questions and *Snow White* itself are no more than a spoof of the "serious" novel designed to be interpreted. "Do you stand up when you read?" he asks, and "In your opinion, should human beings have more shoulders? . . . Two sets of shoulders? . . . Three?" These last questions are as relevant as the first few to a novel that completely resists all attempts at conventional interpretation.

The reader, accustomed to the traditional novel, is left puzzled and faintly irritated by *Snow White*. "But what does it mean?" he is likely to demand. When applied to Barthelme's novel, however, such questions prove not only unanswerable but irrelevant. Like the absurd universe itself, the novel eludes all attempts to discover its "meaning," resists all efforts to find in it a coherent "content."

In the only critical article thus far published on *Snow White*, Peter J. Longleigh, Jr., displays his understanding of

Barthelme's intention. The article appears in *Critique*, one of the more consistently satisfying of the journals devoted to contemporary literature. Included with several serious studies and with no introduction or other editorial apparatus to suggest it is anything but serious, Longleigh's article is actually a hilarious "put-on," a straight-faced parody of contemporary criticism.

After asserting that Barthelme "transcends the ethical and aesthetic art forms of past eras," Longleigh manages to trace the influence on *Snow White* of myth, psychology, sociology, and anthropology, not to mention traditional literature. "Notice that the anti-heroine is named 'Snow White,'" he writes at one point. "Yet she writes 'a dirty poem four pages long.' That a Snow White woman could write a four-page dirty poem was, needless to say, unthinkable during the Victorian epoch; and the myth of pure woman is exploded in this vibrantly styled novel."[17] Myth, too, occurs in the novel as "interpreted" by Longleigh: "And now magnificently Mr. Barthelme has selected his controlling myth, underpinning the contemporary tale with this great archetypal vision, like a figure in the carpet, or rug."[18] And what modern novel would be complete without Freudian overtones: "one of the burning issues in the book is whether or not Snow White has a Castration Complex. . . . Notice that Snow White lives in a world of men. She seems incapable of renunciation and ideal-formation which might resolve her conflicts over the female component in her overall makeup. Secondary Narcissism is the logical outcome. Thus we see that Snow White is having sublimated homosexual relations with the little men."[19]

Longleigh's "study" meets Camp with Camp, parody with parody. Like Barthelme's novel, it debunks the traditional concept of meaning in the novel and, by extension, of conventional interpretation. Yet the fact that Barthelme parodies the "novel-of-meaning" does not mean his book is of a non-serious nature. On the contrary, the very senselessness of Barthelme's novel conveys a kind of sense. Just as the reader who demands a coherent meaning from *Snow White* must remain baffled, so must the individual who searches for meaning in the cosmos remain unsatisfied. To convince the reader of the futility of this search seems Barthleme's intention.

Another novel that depends upon artifice to make a serious statement is James Purdy's *Malcolm*, an early novel of the absurd that resembles *Snow White* in its emulation of the fairy tale. As Thomas Lorch points out, Malcolm, the novel's fourteen-year-old protagonist, parallels the fairy-tale orphan or changeling who turns out to be a prince. He is accepted by the King and Queen, represented in the novel by the Girards, inherits a kingdom, and marries the beautiful princess. Instead of enjoyment, however, Malcolm experiences no emotion at all, finally fading out of the picture altogether. He remains unaffected by his rise as a fairy-tale hero.[20]

Similarly, *Malcolm* resembles the initiation story. At fourteen, Malcolm is near the age that the novice began rites of initiation into primitive tribes.[21] Thrust into a world of experience, Malcolm looks eagerly forward to "beginning life."[22] But experience effects no change in Malcolm. He remains untouched by life, the same at death as when Mr. Cox, the initiatory priest in the novel, found him sitting on the bench early in the novel. Society has failed either to corrupt or to educate him, nor has he changed it.

Neither the fairy tale pattern nor the initiation pattern develops along traditional lines. The reader, who has responded to what he thinks is a familiar pattern in modern literature, discovers his expectations thwarted. Other familiar patterns occur as well. Lorch lists the search for a father, the quest for identity, and the victimization of an innocent by society. Certain other elements suggest social satire and the novel of manners. Yet these patterns remain undeveloped. The result is not the obscuration of meaning, but the generation of meaning. "It is by means of dislocations of traditional or expected modes and the peculiar stylized disorder which results," writes Lorch, "that Purdy leads us to his pervasive vision of radical emptiness."[23]

Purdy's use of stylized language also reflects his meaning.

Saul Maloff has described Purdy's language as "awkward, bare, restrained, not-quite-right, and seemingly struggling for coherence."[24] It is an anti-style in that its matter, its content, finally reveals no meaningful information. Yet its very emptiness and artificiality suggest, as Lorch indicates, the emptiness and artificiality of the characters' lives. Madame Girard, in particular, exemplifies this device. She never merely speaks; she orates. Each appearance is a performance, complete with histrionic gestures and pauses.

> "Sit down," Madame Girard commanded Malcolm *sotto voce.* She continued, closing her eyes again:
> "Why should the rest of the world know plenty, happiness, domestic satisfaction, love—while I am shut out from all these things, deprived of a woman's *human* station in life, turned in upon my own devices, and saddled—" here she opened her eyes directly and immediately upon the tray with the wine bottle, then closed them again—"*saddled* with a husband who knows not whether I am alive or dead, and cares, yes, cares—*dear* Eloisa, I can feel you are shaking your head, so stop!—cares LESS." (131)

Such insincerity of language and action often causes Malcolm, who senses its emptiness, to fall asleep. On a thematic level, the stilted artificiality of the prose reflects the hollow meaninglessness of Purdy's absurd world. Thus artifice and meaning merge.

Purdy and Barthelme are representative of most contemporary absurdist novelists in the special ways they use artifice to convey themes that are quite serious. If, in their camping of certain novelistic conventions, they mock the traditional novel, they do so to rejuvenate and transform it, not to destroy it. They don't reject the novel itself, but the traditional concept of the novel and the world view that produced it and which it reflects. Contemporary novelists of the absurd agree with "death-of-art" critics that reality cannot be depicted and that experience resists the ordering imagination. They also recognize that "reality" and experience comprise the content of most traditional novels. As we have seen, the resulting impasse is met and overcome by the ironic use these novelists make of certain traditional devices. Burlesque, in particular, when used reflexively, allows contemporary absurdist novelists to mock the conventional novel as obsolete while simultaneously employing its conventions in vitally new ways, paradoxically to sing its obsequies and effect its resurrection in a single stroke. It provides them with a method for including in the novel itself what Fiedler calls "the perception of [the novel's] own absurdity, even impossibility,"[25] while at the same time transcending that impossibility to produce "new and original" literature.

Rather than "retire" what Sontag calls "the metaphor of the work of art as a representation of reality,"[26] they exaggerate the metaphor, turning it back upon itself with parody. They consequently suggest disorder by mocking order. Content—meaning—remains, even if that meaning is cosmic meaninglessness. Order remains, if only to mock itself reflexively. Such presentation does not represent, as Mailer contends, "the art of the cannibal," which sups upon its own family, amusing "by the very act of its destruction."[27] To the contrary, the use of artifice by contemporary American novelists of the absurd reinforces meaning, allowing these novelists to infuse the genre with new blood, rescuing it from a host of premature gravediggers.

Like Camp, pop-forms are also frequently adapted to recent absurdist novels. Vonnegut, for example, often emulates science fiction and Utopian-fantasy, and Barth's *The Sot-Weed Factor* has been read as a western.[28] Even pornography, which Fiedler calls "the *essential* form of pop art,"[29] has been adapted for serious purposes, the most famous example of which is perhaps Terry Southern's *Candy*.[30] Another recent example of the adaptation of a pop-form to an absurdist novel in order to make a serious statement is Thomas Berger's *Little Big Man*.

Though ostensibly a comic western, Berger's novel seriously questions the methods by which man records and orders his past. Like *The Sot-Weed Factor*, it burlesques and debunks history. The novel concerns the first thirty-four years in the life of Jack Crabb, whom the Indians name Little Big Man since he stands only slightly above five feet tall. Crabb grows up with the West, living part of the time as an Indian (they "capture" him when he is ten), part of the time as a white man. An occasional buffalo hunter, Crabb witnesses the near extinction of that once plentiful breed. He sees as well the coming of the railroad as it inexorably penetrates the virgin West, not to mention the defeat of the Indians by the United States cavalry. He engages in a gunfight with Wild Bill Hickock, a fistfight with Wyatt Earp, watches a fight between Annie Oakley and his huge sister, Caroline, and is the only survivor of the Little Big Horn massacre.

The reliability of Crabb's story is undercut by the fantastic quality of his tale and by a series of implausible coincidences (Crabb keeps running "accidentally" into long lost members of his family, both Indian and white). But the use of a frame narrator is the primary device by which Berger reduces the tale's reliability. Ralph Fielding Snell, wealthy amateur historian, relates the story as it was told him by a one-hundred-eleven-year-old Jack Crabb, a patient in the psychiatric ward of a state hospital. "I have never been able to decide how much of Mr. Crabb's story to believe," says Snell in his Epilogue to the novel. "Jack Crabb was either the most neglected hero in the history of this country or a liar of insane proportions."[31] The similarity of this narrative frame to the one used by Barth in *Giles Goat-Boy* is obvious. Both lend an air of uncertainty to the several hundreds of pages we have just read in these massive novels, an uncertainty that in both novels forms part of the point.

Snell's problem stems from the fact that Crabb's tale clashes with official records. While certain of Crabb's assertions are verifiable, most are not. Indeed, official "fact" seems to deny Crabb's very existence: "In my library of three thousand volumes of the Old West," writes Snell, "in the hundreds of clippings, letters, magazines, you will search in vain, as I have, for the most fleeting reference to one man, and not a commonplace individual by any means, but by his own account a participant in the pre-eminent events of the most colorful quarter-century on the American frontier. I refer, of course, to *Jack Crabb*" (447). The contradiction between history, on the one hand, and a first-hand account of history given by a man who was there, on the other, casts doubt upon Crabb's veracity to be sure, but also upon the official record. Berger's novel, like *The Sot-Weed Factor*, rejects all rational systems that impose meaning upon a meaningless universe.

Berger also debunks the myth of the Old West and its heroes. In a gun battle, Crabb bests Wild Bill Hickock, who is much larger and a better shot, simply by using his wits, making the legendary hero appear ridiculous. He also regularly beats Hickock in poker, a game at which Hickock's skill is almost as famous as his expert gun-play. Similarly, in Berger's mock-version of the massacre at Little Big Horn, the Indians refuse to scalp Custer, portrayed as an egotistical bully, not because they respect him, but because he is growing bald, losing his legendary yellow hair. History, myth, and Jack Crabb may all be lying, but Berger's novel indicates it would be difficult to determine which is the most flagrant falsehood.

Robert Coover also uses a pop-form seriously to examine the way man imposes order and meaning upon his absurd existence. *The Universal Baseball Association, Inc., J. Henry Waugh, Prop.* (1968) adapts the form of the sports story. It concerns J. Henry Waugh, a lonely middle-aged accountant who has invented a baseball game that is played with dice. The game begins as an innocent enough diversion, but Waugh soon becomes obsessed with it. He creates an entire league, complete with teams and players, official standings and statistics, and charts on which the incidents of each game are found, carefully calculated according to the laws of probability. He follows his imagined players not only on the playing field but into their private lives. They write songs, have love affairs, get drunk, form political parties. Soon Waugh's invented world becomes as real as the world he inhabits. Moreover, it seems to operate independent of his control; the characters take over, leading their own lives. Waugh, the creator of this make-believe world, can only watch, waiting to see what will happen next.

Coover's novel is an extended metaphor, of course. Waugh represents God, the game is the world, and we are the players. Just as modern physics teaches that the world is essentially uncertain and at best probable, so is Waugh's Association governed by the laws of probability he has devised. In the game's history, which Waugh dutifully records in his "Official Archives," things remained exciting for a number of years (Waugh can play several years of baseball games in a few weeks), the period Waugh refers to as the Golden Age. Recently, however, a period of dullness had set in, causing Waugh to consider abandoning the game. Suddenly, in the year LVI, the time at which the novel begins, young Damon Rutherford appears on the scene. In his rookie season, he pitches a perfect game, infusing new life and excitement into the game, promising a new era. Rutherford seems a combination Fisher King and Christ-figure who will redeem us from dullness and keep the "game" interesting.

Certain throws of the dice refer Waugh to the Extraordinary Occurrences Chart which contains rare incidents—such as injuries and deaths—that keep the game exciting and interesting. With Rutherford at bat, the dice refer Waugh to this Chart. Waugh again throws the dice, which to his horror read 1-1-1, a combination meaning death. Rutherford, the hope of the Association, is hit and killed by a pitched ball. Waugh, heart-stricken, considers saving the felled Savior. He could cheat, turn one of the dice over, throw again—but that would violate the rules. Waugh/God doesn't operate that way. "The Proprietor of the Universal Baseball Association, utterly brought down, brought utterly to grief, buried his face in the heap of papers on his kitchen table and cried for a long bad time."[32]

After Rutherford's death, the game—as well as Waugh's private life—begins deteriorating. Waugh takes to drink, suffers insomnia, and finally loses his job. Increasingly, he moves farther and farther away from his world into the world of his game. Yet neither world proves satisfactory:

> So what were his possible strategies? He could quit the game. Burn it. But what would that do to *him*? Odd thing about an operation like this league: once you set it in motion, you were yourself somehow launched into the same orbit; there was growth in the making of it, development, but there was also a defining of the outer edges. Moreover, the urge to annihilate—he'd felt it before—seemed somehow alien to him, and he didn't trust it. And yet: what else could he do?

As Leo J. Hertzel points out, "Since the death of Christ, things haven't gone very well for the world; it must have been a jolt to God."[33]

Coover's point is made explicit in the final chapter of his novel. It occurs years after the death of Damon, who is now worshiped as a Messiah-figure. It is Damonday CLVII, the day on which Rutherford's death is ritualistically re-enacted in what Hertzel calls "a kind of baseballmass."[34] Waugh doesn't appear at all in the chapter. His presence is implied, of course, since the game still goes on, but for the most part he has departed, simply going through the motions of throwing the dice and recording the results.

The players participating in the ritual speculate on the nature of their universe. "I'm afraid," says one, " . . . that God exists and he is a nut" (168). Another, Raspberry Schultz, opines: "I don't know if there's really a record-keeper up there or not. . . . But even if there weren't, I think we'd have to play the game as though there were" (172). And finally, in Coover's version of the world is all that the case is: "It's not a trial, . . . It's not even a lesson. It's just what it is" (174).

The Universal Baseball Association is not a sports story but an extended metaphor of Coover's theme. The world is absurd, its purpose no more coherent than the random throw of dice. The ritualistic reenactment of Damon's death at the novel's close represents a senseless attempt to impose universal significance on an isolated, chance occurrence. "If there's a dice shaker up there," writes Hertzel, "he's ... Waugh whose game was nearly destroyed one night when a drunken friend flooded it with beer. Why did anyone ever think things in another world would be better, stronger, wiser, sterner."[35] Like Berger, Coover adapts a pop-form, not to rid his book of seriousness, but to enhance his statement about the absurd nature of the human condition.

A number of other novels could be cited that display the treatment of absurdist themes with what I have been calling absurdist techniques, techniques that often merge so successfully with content that the two become indissoluble. Bruce Jay Friedman's *Stern* (1962), for example, employs a number of absurdist techniques, particularly during the scene at the Grove Rest Home when Stern, the protagonist, encounters half-men and mechanical men, grotesque symbols of his own feelings of inadequacy and incompleteness. Ken Kesey's first novel, *One Flew Over the Cuckoo's Nest* (1962), also presents an absurdist vision with absurdist techniques. Because Chief Bromden, who narrates the novel, is insane, however, a "psychological" explanation exists for the flat, two-dimensional quality of Kesey's world, serving to lessen the effectiveness of Kesey's burlesque tactics. Other novelists who, in varying degrees, treat absurdist themes with absurdist techniques include Stanley Elkin, Ishmael Reed, Charles Simmons, and Richard Farina. In each case, the artist emphasizes various artifices, including those characteristic of Camp and the pop-novel, in such a way that his absurdist vision receives emphasis and focus, thus enhancing meaning. In the final analysis, the absurdist works themselves, particularly those of Heller, Vonnegut, Pynchon, and Barth, provide the best arguments against death-of-the-novel critics, arguments that are finally unassailable. In the capable hands of contemporary American novelists of the absurd, the old genre continues to function as healthily and as effectively as ever.

Notes and References

Chapter One

1. These theories are discussed rather fully in Wylie Sypher's *Loss of the Self in Modern Literature and Art* (New York, 1962). See also: on modern science, Jacob Bronowski, *The Common Sense of Science* (Cambridge, Mass., 1953) and Sir Edmund Whittaker: *From Euclid to Eddington: A Study of Conceptions of the External World* (New York, 1958); on the "new" logic or anti-logic, Percy W. Bridgman, *The Way Things Are* (Cambridge, Mass., 1959) and Stephane Lupasco, *Logique et Contradiction* (Paris, 1947); the sociological allusions are of course to David Riesman's *The Lonely Crowd* (New Haven, 1950), William Hollingsworth Whyte's *The Organization Man* (New York, 1956), and Paul Goodman's *Growing Up Absurd* (New York, 1960), but see also Erich Fromm's *The Sane Society* (New York, 1955).

2. Quoted in Paul Levine, "The Intemperate Zone: The Climate of Contemporary American Fiction," *Massachusetts Review*, VIII (Summer, 1967), 505-6. See also Howe's "Introduction" to *Literary Modernism* (New York, 1967) and his "Mass Society and Post-Modern Fiction," *Partisan Review*, XXVI (Summer, 1959), 420-36.

3. *Commentary*, XXI (March, 1961), 224.

4. "Anatomy of Black Humor," in *The American Novel Since World War II*, ed. Marcus Klein (New York, 1969), p. 225.

5. New York, 1965.

6. *Time to Murder and Create: The Contemporary Novel in Crisis* (New York, 1966), p. 145.

7. Howe, "Mass Society and Post-Modern Fiction," p. 429. Howe complains that most of the post-war novelists in America "were unable, or perhaps too shrewd, to deal with the postwar experience directly; they preferred tangents of suggestion to frontal representation; they could express their passionate, though often amorphous, criticism of American life not through realistic portraiture but through fable, picaresque, prophecy and nostalgia."

8. Among others, the following have used the term "Black Humor": Bruce Jay Friedman, *op. cit.*; Hamlin Hill, "Black Humor: Its Causes and Cure," *Colorado Quarterly*, XVII (1968), 57-64; "The

Black Humorists," *Time*, February 12, 1965, pp. 94-96; and Max F. Schultz, "Pop, Op, and Black Humor: The Aesthetics of Anxiety," *College English*, XXX (December, 1968), 230-40; "Black comedy" is used by Michael R. French, "The American Novel in the Sixties," *Midwest Quarterly*, IX (July, 1968), 365-79; "affluent terrorism" is Feldman's term, *op. cit.* (above, note 4); Robert Scholes refers to the novels as examples of "Epicurean comedy" in *The Fabulators* (New York, 1967), especially chapter 3; "the psychic novel" is used by Robert Buckeye, "The Anatomy of the Psychic Novel," *Critique*, IX, ii (1967), 33-45; and Alvin Greenburg considers them as "novels of disintegration" in "The Novels of Disintegration: Paradoxical Impossibility in Contemporary Fiction," *Wisconsin Studies in Contemporary Literature*, VII (Winter-Spring, 1966), 103-24. Both Buckeye and Greenburg discuss the European as well as the American novel of the absurd.

9. Ihab Hassan, *Radical Innocence* (New York, 1961); Richard Lehan, "Existentialism in Recent American Fiction: The Demonic Quest," *Texas Studies in Literature and Language*, I (Summer, 1959), 181-202.

10. *The Theater of the Absurd* (New York, 1961), pp. xix-xx.

11. "The Point Is That There Isn't Any Point," *The New York Times Book Review*, June 6, 1965, p. 28.

12. *Ernest Hemingway* (Minneapolis, 1965), revised edition, p. 13.

13. *Ibid.*, p. 38.

14. "The Absurd Style in Contemporary American Literature," *Humanities Association Bulletin*, XIX (Spring, 1968), 44-45.

15. *The Atlantic* , CCXX (August, 1967), 33.

16. *Ibid.*, p. 31. It is interesting to note that Beckett's most recent work, a play entitled *Breath*, runs only thirty seconds and contains no dialogue or characters at all. For a thorough examination of the "literature of silence," see Ihab Hassan's *The Literature of Silence: Henry Miller and Samuel Beckett* (New York, 1967).

17. *Ibid.*

18. *Ibid.*

19. *No! In Thunder* (Boston, 1960), p. 11.

20. In an interview, Barth comments on the "imitative" quality of the new novel. "From what I know of Robbe-Grillet and his pals," he says, "their aesthetic is finally a more up-to-date kind of psychological realism; a higher fi to human consciousness and unconsciousness." In John Enck, "John Barth: An Interview," *Wisconsin Studies in Contemporary Literature*, VI (Winter-Spring, 1965), 5-6. Esslin places the Theater of the Absurd with the "anti-literary movement of our time, which has found its expression in abstract painting with its rejection of 'literary' elements in pictures; or in the 'new novel' in France, with its reliance on the description of objects and its rejection of empathy and anthropomorphism" (*The Theatre of the Absurd*, p. xxi).

21. There are a few exceptions, of course, particularly in Pynchon's *V.* and Heller's *Catch-22.* But even in these novels, distortion is occasional and never so extreme as the "grotesqueries of modern theater" Karl S. Guthke lists in his *Modern Tragicomedy: An Investigation into the Nature of the Genre* (New York, 1966). Guthke provides the following catalogue:

> ... legless people live in garbage cans (Beckett's *Endgame*); an ugly woman is shot and thereby transformed into a beautiful princess (Ionesco's *The Picture*); a rare disease, rhinoceritis, turns people into rhinoceroses (Ionesco's *Rhinocéros*); in a grotesque brothel it is not beyond the girls to discard, along with their clothes, their cheeks, eyes, and other parts of the body until only the skeleton remains (Jean Tardieu's *La Serrure* [*The Lock*]); the dead arise (Tardieu's *Qui est là?* [*Who Is There?*]); people are transformed into works of art and packed in boxes to be shipped (Wolfgang Hildesheimer's *Landschaft mit Figurer* [*Landscape with Figures*]); or they can have coins for eyes, the mouthpiece of a telephone for a mouth, and an antenna-equipped radio for a forehead (Ivan Goll's *Methusalem*) (pp. 74-75).

22. "Barth: An Interview," p. 6.

23. "The Literature of Exhaustion," p. 31.

24. See Russel H. Miller, "The Sot-Weed Factor: A Contemporary Mock-Epic," *Critique*, VIII (Winter, 1965-66), 88-100; Tony Tanner, "The Hoax That Joke Bilked," *Partisan Review*, XXXIV (Winter, 1967), 102-9, who sees *The Sot-Weed Factor* as a parody of the picaresque novel; and Constance Denniston, "The American Romance Parody: A Study of Purdy's *Malcolm* and Heller's *Catch-22*," *Emporia State Research Studies*, XIV, ii, 42-45, 63-64.

25. "Anatomy of the Psychic Novel," p. 37.

26. Jacob Bronowski, *op. cit.*, explains the evolution from the eighteenth-century idea of an ordered universe to the nineteenth-century idea of a universe functioning according to cause and effect mechanics to the present idea of a universe ruled by chance. In science today, Bronowski writes, "every description of nature contains some essential and irremovable uncertainty" (p. 67).

27. "The Point Is That There Isn't Any Point," p. 28.

28. "Anatomy of the Psychic Novel," p. 37.

29. In parodying the eighteenth-century novel, for example, Barth's *The Sot-Weed Factor* implicitly parodies the eighteenth-century view that the universe was well ordered. See Martin C. Battestin's analysis of *Tom Jones* as a reflection of a divinely ordered universe, the art of the novel implying the art of God, in his "Introduction," *Twentieth Century Interpretations of Tom Jones* (Englewood Cliffs, N.J., 1968), pp. 10-14.

30. "Literature of Exhaustion," p. 31.

31. "Absurd Style in Contemporary American Literature," p. 45; Leslie Fiedler, *The Return of the Vanishing American* (New York, 1968), p. 184.

32. Fiedler, *Ibid.*

33. "The Intemperate Zone," pp. 514-19. Among the novels Levine includes as "neorealistic" are Burroughs' *Naked Lunch*, Rechy's *City of Night*, Hubert Selby, Jr.'s *Last Exit to Brooklyn*, and Capote's *In Cold Blood*. Levine defines Neorealism as "an attempt to photograph the unreality of modern life through an objective camera eye . . . " (519).

34. New York, 1962, p. 34.

35. "Absurd Style in Contemporary American Literature," p. 45.

36. *The Theatre of the Absurd*, p. 304.

37. Aldridge's comments on the journalistic style seem relevant here. "Through journalism [the novelist] is able to present material without taking an attitude toward it or judging its significance. . . . If for one moment the events chosen cease to be important or the reader, having been exposed to too many events, ceases to react to them, then the writer is thrown into a dilemma from which only greater talent than he possesses can possibly free him." From "The Search for Values," in *The American Novel Since World War II*, p. 47.

38. *The Fabulators*, p. 41.

39. *Shakespeare Our Contemporary*, trans. Boleslaw Taborski (Garden City, N.Y., 1964), p. 92.

40. Kott, pp. 92-93 (italics mine).

41. *Ibid.*, p. 91.

42. Quoted in Esslin, p. 133.

43. *The Fabulators*, p. 43 (italics mine).

44. Esslin, p. 316.

45. "France and America: Versions of the Absurd," *College English*, XXVI (May, 1965), 635 (italics mine).

46. An exception is Heller, who seems to place a certain faith in Yossarian's ability to escape his absurd circumstances in *Catch-22*.

47. "Writing American Fiction," p. 231.

Chapter Two

1. Oct. 27, 1961, p. 97.

2. *The New York Times Book Review*, Oct. 22, 1961, p. 50.

3. Dec. 9, 1961, p. 147.

4. *The New Republic*, Nov. 13, 1961, pp. 13, 11.

5. *The New York Times*, Oct. 23, 1961, p. 27.

6. See Brian Way, "Formal Experiment and Social Discontent: Joseph Heller's *Catch-22*," *American Studies*, II (Oct., 1968), 253.

7. *The Power Elite* (New York, 1956).

8. Way, p. 257.

9. *Ibid.*

10. John Enck, "John Barth: An Interview," *Wisconsin Studies in Contemporary Literature*, VI (Winter-Spring, 1965), 13.

11. Joseph Heller, *Catch-22* (New York, 1961), p. 164. Subsequent page references will be from this volume and will be noted

parenthetically in the text. Quoted by permission of the publisher.

12. *"Catch-22: Déjà vu* and the Labyrinth of Memory," *Bucknell Review*, XVI (May, 1968), 35.

13. "Joseph Heller's *Catch-22*: Only Fools Walk in Darkness," in *Contemporary American Novelists*, ed. Harry T. Moore (Carbondale, Ill., 1966), p. 140.

14. "Formal Experiment and Social Discontent," p. 264.

15. "Heller's *Catch-22*: Protest of a *Puer Eternis*," *Critique*, VII (Winter, 1964-65), 150-62.

16. "Structure of *Catch-22*," *Critique*, IX, ii (1967), 47-48.

17. "I See Everything Twice!: The Structure of Joseph Heller's *Catch-22*," *University Review*, XXXIV (Spring, 1968), 177.

18. "Déjà vu and the Labyrinth of Memory," p. 36.

19. "Formal Experiment and Social Discontent," p. 267.

20. Way, p. 267.

21. Solomon, p. 52.

22. Way, p. 267.

23. Karl, "Only Fools Walk in Darkness," p. 141.

24. *A Reader's Guide to William Faulkner* (New York, 1964), pp. 355-77.

Chapter Three

1. Mark R. Hillegas, *The Future as Nightmare: H. G. Wells and the Anti-Utopians* (New York, 1967), considers Vonnegut as a science fiction writer. Bruce Jay Friedman, *Black Humor* (New York, 1965), sees him as a "black humorist," and R. Z. Shepherd, *Life*, April 8, 1966, p. 15, calls him a satirist.

2. Hillegas, p. 159.

3. *Player Piano* was published by Scribner's in 1952, *Sirens* by Dell in 1959, and *Mother Night* and *Canary* by Fawcett in 1961, all in paperback.

4. "Kurt Vonnegut, Head Bokononist," *The New York Times Book Review* April 6, 1969, p. 2.

5. Robert Scholes, " 'Mirthridates, he died old': Black Humor and Kurt Vonnegut, Jr.," *Hollins Critic*, III, vi, 1-12, reprinted in Scholes' *The Fabulators* (New York, 1967). Carlo Pagetts, "Kurt Vonnegut, tra fanta scienza e utopia," *Studi Americani*, XII (1968), 307-22.

6. "Cross the Border, Close the Gap," *Playboy*, XVI (Dec., 1969), 230.

7. Bryan, p. 2.

8. Fiedler, p. 253.

9. Bryan, p. 2.

10. *Ibid.*

11. *Ibid.*

12. Fiedler, p. 252.

13. *Ibid.*

14. *Mother Night* (New York, 1966), p. 103. The hardbound rather than the original paperback edition is used here. No changes in the text of the original occur in the hardbound edition, but an introduction has been added. Further quotations will be noted parenthetically in the text.

15. Jean-Paul Sartre, "Existentialism is a Humanism."

16. "Law, Morality, and Individual Rights," in *Readings for Rhetoric*, ed. by Frederick P. Kroeger, *et al.* (Belmont, California, 1969), p. 317.

17. *God Bless You, Mr. Rosewater, or Pearls Before Swine* (New York, 1965), p. 47. Further quotations from this edition will be noted parenthetically in the text.

18. In *Mother Night*, Vonnegut also mentions this theme. He writes: "No young person on earth is so excellent in all respects as to need no uncritical love. Good Lord—as youngsters play their parts in political tragedies with casts of billions, uncritical love is the only real treasure they can look for" (44).

19. "Law, Morality, and Individual Rights," p. 317.

20. Such moral squeamishness appears less exaggerated when one considers the recent action of a Las Vegas police chief. Informed that the rock-musical *Hair*, which contains a nude scene, planned to open in Las Vegas, he issued an order that public revelation of pubic hair would result in immediate arrests.

21. While treated sympathetically, Harry is no normative character. As his name suggests, Harry Pena is a burlesque-figure also. Vonnegut is making fun of the excessively masculine stance.

22. Albert Camus, *Le Mythe de Sisyphe* (Paris, 1942), p. 18.

23. (New York, 1959). All quotations will be from this edition and will be noted parenthetically in the text.

24. (New York, 1963). All quotations will be from this edition and will be noted parenthetically in the text.

25. "Utopias in Negative," *Sewanee Review*, LXIV (Winter, 1956), 85.

26. Hillegas, p. 9.

27. *Ibid.*, p. 8.

28. Anti-utopian novelists often portray a state much like that envisioned by H. G. Wells. But the result of the Utopias they portray is not human happiness, as Wells envisioned, but human misery and uselessness. Hillegas elaborates this point fully in his excellent study.

29. (New York, 1969), pp. 87-88.

30. "Black Comedy with Purifying Laughter," *Harper's*, CCXXXII (May, 1966), 15.

31. (New York, 1968), p. xiv.

32. Burton Feldman, "Anatomy of Black Humor," in *The American Novel Since World War II*, ed. Marcus Klein (New York, 1969), p. 224.

33. By suggesting "Divine appointment," Vonnegut burlesques

the Jonah-theme. This theme also occurs in *Cat's Cradle*, the protagonist of which believes that "Somebody or something has compelled me to be certain places at certain times, without fail" (11). But whereas the biblical Jonah performs a divine mission, saving the city of Ninevah from divinely inspired destruction by converting its inhabitants, Eliot Rosewater reforms no one, and the Jonah of *Cat's Cradle* succeeds only in securing a front-row seat for doomsday.

34. *The Fabulators*, pp. 136-37.

35. Vonnegut also burlesques the conventional novel with his comic use of chapters. In *Cat's Cradle*, a novel of less than two-hundred pages, for example, Vonnegut includes one-hundred-twenty-seven chapters.

Chapter Four

1. "My Confession," in *The Living Thoughts of Tolstoy*, ed. by Stefan Zweig (New York, 1963), p. 46.

2. *Time in Literature* (Berkeley, 1955), p. 65.

3. Kenneth E. Boulding, *The Meaning of the 20th Century: The Great Transition* (New York, 1965), p. 139.

4. *The Human Use of Human Beings: Cybernetics and Society* (New York, 1954), p. 20.

5. *Kenyon Review*, XXII (Winter, 1960), 277-92. Subsequent references to "Entropy" appear parenthetically in my text.

6. *The Common Sense of Science* (Cambridge, Mass., 1953), p. 67.

7. Thomas Pynchon, *V.* (Philadelphia, 1963), pp. 290-91. Subsequent references to *V.* appear in parentheses following the quotation.

8. "Comic Escape and Anti-Vision: The Novels of Joseph Heller and Thomas Pynchon," in *Adversity and Grace: Studies in Recent American Literature*, ed. by Nathan A. Scott, Jr. (Chicago, 1968), p. 98.

9. "Comic Escape and Anti-Vision," p. 98.

10. *Ibid.*, pp. 103-4.

11. *Human Use of Human Beings*, p. 130.

12. Sigmund Freud, *Collected Papers*, ed. J. Riviere and J. Strachey, vol. 5 (New York, 1924-50), p. 345.

13. *Loss of the Self in Modern Literature and Art* (New York, 1962), p. 73.

14. Norman O. Brown, *Life Against Death* (New York, 1959), p. 88.

15. Hunt notes a proliferation of "images of the female being ravished by the inanimate" in *V.*; other than Melanie's impalement, he lists " 'Malta . . . a noun feminine' lying on her back, 'an immemorial woman. Spread to the explosive orgasms of Mussolini bombs' (p. 318); Foppl with the Herero girl; Melanie's self-ravishment with a mannequin beneath a mirror." In "Comic Escape and Anti-Vision," p. 105.

16. If Stencil is correct in this diagnosis, it becomes possible that

all the events in the novel ordered by his imagination are colored by his submerged death wish. This possibility adds yet another dimension to the uncertainty of the novel.

17. Dance of Death allusions also occur on pages 244, 262, and 264.

18. "Thomas Pynchon's Multiple Absurdities," *Wisconsin Studies in Contemporary Literature*, VII (Autumn, 1966), 266.

19. *From Euclid to Eddington: A Study of Conceptions of the External World* (New York, 1958), p. 45.

20. It is interesting that in Victoria Wren, whose "element" is riot and whose room creeps "with amassed objects" (487), the two extremes, The Street and The Hothouse with all their range of meanings, converge.

21. P. 58.

22. Wiener, p. 31.

23. *Ibid.*, p. 125.

24. *Ibid.*, p. 67.

25. *Ibid.*, p. 70.

26. *The Art of Loving* (New York, 1963), p. 72.

27. *Human Use of Human Beings*, p. 72.

28. *The Crying of Lot-49* (Philadelphia, 1966), p. 181. Subsequent references to the novel appear in parentheses following the quotation.

29. Wiener, pp. 41-44.

Chapter Five

1. "The Point Is That There Isn't Any Point," *The New York Times Book Review*, June 6, 1965, p. 28.

2. "The Novel as Parody," *Critique*, VI (Fall, 1963), 85.

3. "The Virgin Laureate," *Time*, September 5, 1960, p. 77; "The Joke Is On Mankind," *The New York Times Book Review*, August 21, 1960, p. 4; and *"The Sot-Weed Factor*: A Contemporary Mock Epic," *Critique*, VIII (Winter-Spring, 1965-66), 88, 100.

4. "'I' Faith, 'Tis Good," *Newsweek*, August 29, 1960, p. 89.

5. Leslie Fiedler, "John Barth: An Eccentric Genius," *The New Leader*, Feb., 13, 1961, p. 23.

6. Harris Dientsfrey, "Blended Especially for a Heady Smoke," *Book Week*, March 15, 1965, p. 18.

7. XLII (Oct., 1966), 89-95.

8. "The Literature of Exhaustion," in *The American Novel Since World War II*, ed. by Marcus Klein (New York, 1969), p. 274.

9. *Ibid.*, p. 269.

10. Quoted in *Newsweek*, August 8, 1966, p. 82.

11. *Ibid.*

12. *Ibid.*

13. "The Literature of Exhaustion," p. 275.

14. *Ibid.*

15. *Ibid.*, pp. 275-77.

16. *The Sot-Weed Factor*, rev. ed. (New York, 1967), p. 126. Subsequent references to *The Sot-Weed Factor* will be entered parenthetically in my text following the quotations.

17. *The End of the Road*, rev. ed. (New York, 1967), p. 112. Subsequent references to *The End of the Road* will be entered parenthetically in my text following the quotations.

18. "John Barth and the Novel of Comic Nihilism," *Wisconsin Studies in Contemporary Literature*, VII (Autumn, 1966), 251.

19. "The Hoax That Joke Bilked," *Partisan Review*, XXXIV (Winter, 1967), 105.

20. "Existence not only precedes essence," Barth writes in *The End of the Road*; "in the case of human beings it rather defies essence" (122).

21. *The Fabulators* (New York, 1967), p. 420.

22. As Scholes points out, *ibid.*, "It is no wonder that when [George] emerges from WESCAC's belly he wears the mask of Harold Bray. Like Bray, he has not Answers to offer, but empty rhetoric."

23. *The Fabulators*, p. 167.

24. "Barth: An Interview," p. 12.

25. *The Hero With A Thousand Faces* (Cleveland, 1956), p. 58.

26. *Ibid.*, p. 69.

27. *Ibid.*, p. 73.

28. *Ibid.*, p. 77.

29. *Ibid.*, p. 98.

30. *Ibid.*, pp. 90-94.

31. *Ibid.*, p. 248.

32. *Ibid.*, p. 153.

33. *Ibid.*, p. 39.

34. *Ibid.*, p. 154.

35. *Ibid.*, p. 40.

36. "In three words Max Spielman synthesized all the fields which thitherto he'd browsed in brilliantly one by one—showed the 'sphincter's riddle' and the mystery of the University to be the same. *Ontogeny recapitulates cosmogeny*—what is it but to say that proctoscopy repeats hagiography? That our Founder on Founder's Hill and the rawest freshman on his first *mons veneris* are father and son? That my day, my year, my life, and the history of West Campus are wheels within wheels?" (7)

37. *The Hero With A Thousand Faces*, pp. 116, 120.

38. *Ibid.*, p. 120

39. *Ibid.*, p. 131.

40. *Newsweek*, p. 82.

41. *The Hero With A Thousand Faces*. p. 193.

42. *Ibid.*, p. 218.

43. "The Literature of Exhaustion," p. 278.

44. "Barth: An Interview," p. 6.

45. See especially *The Fabulators*, pp. 145-73.

46. "Barth: An Interview," p. 13.

47. *Ibid.*, p. 7.

48. "The Pride of Lemuel Gulliver," *The Sewanee Review*, LXIII (Winter, 1955), 54-55.

49. "Introduction," *Twentieth Century Interpretations of Tom Jones*, ed. by Martin C. Battestin (Englewood Cliffs, N.J., 1968), p. 11.

50. *Ibid.*, p. 12.

51. In the Enck interview, *op. cit.*, Barth says he outlines his novels "very thoroughly. ... I don't see how anybody starts a novel without knowing how it's going to end. I usually make detailed outlines: how many chapters it will be and so forth." Pp. 6-7.

52. Battestin, pp. 12-13.

53. *The Rhetoric of Fiction* (Chicago, 1961), pp. 215-18.

54. Quoted in Richard W. Murphy, "In Print: John Barth," *Horizon*, V (Jan., 1963), 37.

55. Barth comments upon the preponderance of coincidence in an absurd world in *The Floating Opera*: "Nature, coincidence, can often be a heavy-handed symbolizer. She seems at times fairly to club one over the head with significance. ... One is constantly being confronted with a sun that bursts from behind the clouds just as the home team takes the ball; ominous rumblings of thunder when one is brooding ... ; magnificent sunrises on days when one has resolved to mend one's ways; ... Race Streets marked SLOW; Cemetery Avenues marked ONE WAY. The man ... whose palate is attuned to subtler dishes, can only smile uncomfortably and walk away, reminding himself, if he is wise, that good taste is, after all, only a human invention" (New York, 1956), pp. 116-17.

56. "John Barth as a Novelist of Ideas: The Themes of Value and Identity," *Critique*, VIII (Winter, 1965-66), 103.

57. *Ibid.*, p. 115.

Chapter Six

1. "Cross the Border, Close the Gap," *Playboy*, XVI (Dec., 1969), 230.

2. "The Curious Death of the Novel: or, What to do About Tired Literary Critics," in *The Curious Death of the Novel: Essays in American Literature* (Baton Rouge, 1967), p. 6.

3. "Against Interpretation," in *Against Interpretation* (New York, 1969), p. 15.

4. *Ibid.*

5. "Nathalie Sarraute and the Novel," *ibid.*, p. 118.

6. "The Curious Death of the Novel," p. 20.

7. "Notes on 'Camp,'" *op. cit.*, p. 289.

8. *Ibid.*

9. *Cannibals and Christians* (New York, 1966), p. 101.

10. "Cross the Border, Close the Gap," p. 253.

11. *Ibid.*, p. 252.

12. *Ibid.*

13. *Ibid.*, p. 256.

14. *Ibid.*, p. 252.

15. On this latter point, see David Galloway, *The Absurd Hero in American Fiction* (Austin, 1966). The novel, Galloway argues, "represent[s] a kind of revolt in favor of order. . . . By selecting and rearranging elements from reality and composing them into an imaginative pattern the artist gives them a meaningfulness and a coherence which they would otherwise not have possessed. As an imaginative recreation of experience the novel can thus, in and of itself, become a revolt against a world which appears to have no logical pattern" (p. 7).

16. *Man's Rage for Chaos* (Philadelphia and New York, 1965), p. 34.

17. Peter J. Longleigh, Jr., "Donald Barthelme's *Snow White*," *Critique*, XII, iii (1969), 32.

18. *Ibid.*, pp. 33-34.

19. *Ibid.*, p. 34.

20. "Purdy's *Malcolm*: A Unique Vision of Radical Emptiness," *Wisconsin Studies in Contemporary Literature*, VI (Summer, 1965), 206-7.

21. See Bettina Schwarzschild, "The Forsaken: James Purdy's *Malcolm*," *Texas Quarterly*, X (Spring, 1967), 170-77.

22. (New York, 1959), p. 27.

23. "A Unique Vision of Radical Emptiness," p. 205. Cf., the comments by Beverly Gross on Barth's *Giles Goat-Boy* in "The Anti-Novels of John Barth," *Chicago Review*, XX (November, 1968), 100-1. Miss Gross also detects a number of undeveloped literary patterns in Barth's novel. In the last analysis, Gross concludes, "the book exists to confute expectations. That is its greatest irritation as well as . . . the source of both its meaning and meaninglessness."

24. "James Purdy's Fictions: The Quality of Despair," *Critique*, VI (Spring, 1963), 111-12.

25. "Cross the Border, Close the Gap," p. 252.

26. "Nathalie Sarraute and the Novel," p. 116.

27. *Cannibals and Christians*, pp. 101-2.

28. See Leslie Fiedler, *The Return of the Vanishing American* (New York, 1968).

29. "Cross the Border, Close the Gap," p. 254.

30. For a discussion of the serious side of *Candy*, see David Galloway, "Clown and Saint: The Hero in Current American Fiction," *Critique*, VII (Spring-Summer, 1965), 46-65.

31. *Little Big Man* (New York, 1965), pp. 446-47. Subsequent references to this edition are included parenthetically in the text.

32. *The Universal Baseball Association, Inc., J. Henry Waugh, Prop.* (New York, 1969), p. 59.

33. "What's Wrong With the Christians?" *Critique*, XII, iii (1969), 22.

34. *Ibid.*

35. *Ibid.*, p. 22.

Bibliography

I. PRIMARY SOURCES: In addition to the novels discussed in this study, I have included below a representative sampling of contemporary novels that display, in varying degrees, some of the methods characteristic of contemporary novels of the absurd. Short story collections have been included when they similarly display absurdist themes and techniques.

Barth, John. *The Floating Opera*. New York: Appleton, Century, Crofts, Inc., 1956.
————. *The End of the Road*. New York: Doubleday and Co., 1958.
————. *The Sot-Weed Factor*. New York: Doubleday and Co., 1960.
————. *Giles Goat-Boy*. New York: Doubleday and Co., 1966.
————. *Lost in the Fun House*. New York: Doubleday and Co., 1968. [short stories]
Barthelme, Donald. *Come Back, Doctor Caligari*. New York: Little, Brown and Co., 1964. [short stories]
————. *Snow White*. New York: Atheneum, 1967.
————. *Unspeakable Practices, Unnatural Acts*. New York: Farrar, Straus, and Giroux, 1968. [short stories]
————. *City Life*. New York: Farrar, Straus, and Giroux, 1970. [short stories]
Berger, Thomas. *Reinhart in Love*. New York: Ballantine, 1968.
————. *Crazy in Berlin*. New York: Ballantine, 1968.
————. *Little Big Man*. New York: Dial Press, 1964.
————. *Killing Time*. New York: Dial Press, 1967.
Coover, Robert. *The Origin of the Brunists*. New York: Putnam, 1966.
————. *The Universal Baseball Association, Inc., J. Henry Waugh, Prop.* New York: Random House, 1968.
————. *Pricksongs and Descants*. New York: E. P. Dutton and Co., 1969. [short stories]
Elkin, Stanley. *Boswell, a Modern Comedy*. New York: Random House, 1964.

————. *A Bad Man.* New York: Random House, 1967.

————. *Criers and Kibitzers, Kibitzers and Criers.* New York: Random House, 1966. [short stories]

Farina, Richard. *Been Down So Long It Looks Like Up to Me.* New York: Random House, 1966.

————. *Long Time Coming and a Long Time Gone.* New York: Random House, 1969. [collected stories and prose]

Friedman, Bruce Jay. *Stern.* New York: Simon and Schuster, 1962.

————. *Far From the City of Class.* New York: Simon and Schuster, 1963. [short stories]

————. *A Mother's Kisses.* New York: Simon and Schuster, 1964.

————. *Black Angels.* New York: Simon and Schuster, 1966. [short stories]

Heller, Joseph. *Catch-22.* New York: Simon and Schuster, 1961.

Kesey, Ken. *One Flew Over the Cuckoo's Nest.* New York: Viking Press, 1962.

————. *Sometimes a Great Notion.* New York: Viking Press, 1964.

Pynchon, Thomas. *V.* Philadelphia: J. B. Lippincott Co., 1963.

————. *The Crying of Lot-49.* Philadelphia: J. B. Lippincott Co., 1966.

Purdy, James. *Color of Darkness and Children Is All.* New York: Avon Books, 1965. [short stories]

————. *Malcolm.* New York: Farrar, Straus, and Giroux, 1959.

————. *The Nephew.* New York: Farrar, Straus, and Giroux, 1960.

————. *Cabot Wright Begins.* New York: Farrar, Straus, and Giroux, 1964.

————. *Eustace Chisholm and the Works.* New York: Farrar, Straus, and Giroux, 1967.

Reed, Ishmael. *Free Lance Pallbearers.* New York: Doubleday and Co., 1967.

————. *Yellow Back Radio Broke-Down.* New York: Doubleday and Co., 1969.

Simmons, Charles. *Powdered Eggs.* New York: E. P. Dutton and Co., Inc., 1964.

Vonnegut, Kurt, Jr. *Player Piano.* New York: Holt, Rinehart, and Winston, 1966.

————. *Sirens of Titan.* New York: Houghton, Mifflin Co., 1961.

————. *Canary in a Cat House.* New York: Fawcett Publications, Inc., 1961. [short stories]

————. *Mother Night.* New York: Harper and Row, 1966.

————. *Cat's Cradle.* New York: Holt, Rinehart, and Winston, 1963.

————. *God Bless You, Mr. Rosewater, or Pearls Before Swine.* New York: Holt, Rinehart, and Winston, 1965.

————. *Welcome to the Monkey House.* New York: Delacorte Press, 1968. [short stories]

————. *Slaughterhouse-Five, or the Children's Crusade*. New York: Delacorte, 1969.

II. SECONDARY SOURCES: I have divided this section into three categories. The first category contains only those books consulted in the preparation of this study and includes books that deal with extra-literary as well as literary matters. The second category is restricted to articles that have appeared in professional literary journals. Since many of these articles concern a number of different absurdist novels, I have chosen not to further subdivide the category by novels or novelists. The final category lists reviews and articles that have appeared in journals of a non-professional nature. It is highly selective, including only those materials that touch in some way upon the concerns of this study.

A. *Books*

Aldridge, John W. *Time to Murder and Create: The Contemporary Novel in Crisis*. New York: David McKay Co., Inc., 1956.

Angrist, Stanley W. and Loren G. Helper. *Order and Chaos: Laws of Energy and Entropy*. New York: Basic Books, Inc., 1967.

Battestin, Martin J., ed. *Twentieth-Century Interpretations of Tom Jones*. Englewood Cliffs, N.J.: Prentice-Hall, Inc., 1968.

Battino, Rubin and Scott E. Wood. *Thermodynamics: An Introduction*. New York: Academic Press, 1968.

Baumbach, Jonathan. *The Landscape of Nightmare: Studies in the Contemporary American Novel*. New York: New York University Press, 1965.

Bergson, Henri; George Meredith, and Wylie Sypher. *Comedy*. Garden City: Anchor Books, 1956.

Bier, Jesse. *The Rise and Fall of American Humor*. New York: Holt, Rinehart, and Winston, 1968.

Booth, Wayne. *The Rhetoric of Fiction*. Chicago: University of Chicago Press, 1961.

Boulding, Kenneth E. *The Meaning of the Twentieth-Century: The Great Transition*. New York: Harper and Row, 1965.

Bridgman, Percy W. *The Way Things Are*. Cambridge, Mass.: Harvard University Press, 1959.

Bronowski, Jacob. *The Common Sense of Science*. Cambridge, Mass.: Harvard University Press, 1953.

Brown, Norman O. *Life Against Death: The Psychoanalytical Meaning of History*. New York: Vintage Books, 1959.

Campbell, Joseph. *The Hero With a Thousand Faces*. Cleveland: The World Publishing Co., 1956.

Camus, Albert. *Le Mythe de Sisyphe*. Paris: Gallimard, 1942.

Davis, Douglas M., ed. *The World of Black Humor*. New York: E. P. Dutton paperback, 1967.

Elliott, Robert C. *The Power of Satire: Magic, Ritual, Art*. Princeton: Princeton University Press, 1960.

Esslin, Martin. *The Theatre of the Absurd.* New York: Anchor Books, 1961.

Fiedler, Leslie. *No! In Thunder.* Boston: Beacon Press, 1960.

―――. *The Return of the Vanishing American.* New York: Stein and Day, 1968.

Friedman, Bruce Jay, ed. *Black Humor.* New York: Bantam Books, Inc., 1965.

Fromm, Erich. *The Art of Loving.* New York: Bantam Books, Inc., 1963.

―――. *The Sane Society.* New York: Rinehart and Co., 1955.

Frye, Northrop. *Anatomy of Criticism: Four Essays.* Princeton: Princeton University Press, 1957.

Galloway, David D. *The Absurd Hero in American Fiction.* Austin: University of Texas Press, 1966.

Goodman, Paul. *Growing Up Absurd.* New York: Random House, 1960.

Grossvogel, David. *Limits of the Novel: Evolution of a Form from Chaucer to Robbe-Grillet.* Ithaca: Cornell University Press, 1968.

Guthke, Karl S. *Modern Tragicomedy: An Investigation Into the Nature of the Genre.* New York: Random House, 1966.

Hassan, Ihab. *Radical Innocence.* New York: Harper and Row, 1966.

―――. *The Literature of Silence: Henry Miller and Samuel Beckett.* New York: Alfred A. Knopf, 1967.

Highet, Gilbert. *The Anatomy of Satire.* Princeton: Princeton University Press, 1962.

Hillegas, Mark R. *The Future as Nightmare: H. G. Wells and the Anti-Utopians.* New York: Oxford University Press, 1967.

Howe, Irving, ed. *Literary Modernism.* New York: Fawcett Publications, 1967.

Kauffman, Walter, ed. *Existentialism from Dostoevsky to Sartre.* Cleveland: Meridian Books, 1956.

Kernan, Alvin. *The Plot of Satire.* New Haven: Yale University Press, 1965.

Klein, Marcus, ed. *The American Novel Since World War II.* New York: Fawcett Publications, 1969.

Kostelanetz, Richard, ed. *On Contemporary Literature.* New York: Avon Books, 1964.

Kott, Jan. *Shakespeare Our Contemporary.* Garden City: Doubleday and Co., 1964.

Kroeger, Frederick P., *et al.*, ed. *Readings for Rhetoric.* Belmont, Cal.: Wadsworth Publishing Co., Inc., 1969.

Langford, Richard E., ed. *Essays in Modern American Literature.* Deland, Fla.: Stetson University Press, 1963.

Lynn, Kenneth S., ed. *The Comic Tradition in America.* Garden City: Anchor Books, 1958.

Mailer, Norman. *Cannibals and Christians.* New York: The Dial Press, 1966.

Malin, Irving. *New American Gothic*. Carbondale: Southern Illinois University Press, 1962.

Meyerhoff, Hans. *Time in Literature*. Berkeley: University of California Press, 1955.

Miller, James E. *Quests Surd and Absurd: Essays in American Literature*. Chicago: University of Chicago Press, 1967.

Mills, C. Wright. *The Power Elite*. New York: Oxford University Press, 1956.

Moore, Harry T., ed. *Contemporary American Novelists*. Carbondale: Southern Illinois University Press, 1967.

O'Connor, William Van. *The Grotesque: An American Genre and Other Essays*. Carbondale: Southern Illinois University Press, 1962.

Peckham, Morse. *Man's Rage for Chaos: Biology, Behavior, and the Arts*. Philadelphia: Chilton Books, 1965.

Rice, Joseph A. *Flash of Darkness: Black Humor in the Contemporary American Novel*. Unpublished Ph.D. dissertation, Florida State University, 1967.

Riesman, David. *The Lonely Crowd*. New York: Yale University Press, 1950.

Rubin, Louis D., Jr. *The Curious Death of the Novel: Essays in American Literature*. Baton Rogue: Louisiana State University Press, 1967.

Scholes, Robert. *The Fabulators*. New York: Oxford University Press, 1967.

————. ed. *Learners and Discerners: A Newer Criticism*. Charlottesville: University Press of Virginia, 1964.

Schulz, Max F. *Radical Sophistication: Studies in Contemporary Jewish-American Novelists*. Athens: Ohio University Press, 1969.

Scott, Nathan, ed. *Adversity and Grace: Studies in Recent American Literature*. Chicago: University of Chicago Press, 1968.

————. *Craters of the Spirit: Studies in the Modern American Novel*. Washington: Corpus Books, 1968.

Sontag, Susan. *Against Interpretation*. New York: Dell Publishing Co., 1969.

Styan, J. L. *Dark Comedy: Development of Modern Comic Tragedy*. New York: Cambridge University Press, 1962.

Sypher, Wylie. *Loss of the Self in Modern Literature and Art*. New York: Vintage Books, 1964.

West, Paul. *The Wine of Absurdity*. University Park, Pa.: Pennsylvania State University Press, 1966.

Whitehead, T. B., ed. *Seven Contemporary Authors*. Austin: University of Texas Press, 1966.

Whittaker, Sir Edmund. *From Euclid to Eddington: A Study of Conceptions of the External World*. New York: Dover Publications, Inc., 1958.

Whyte, William Hollingsworth. *Organization Man.* New York: Simon and Schuster, 1956.

Wiener, Norbert. *Cybernetics: or Control and Communications in the Animal and the Machine.* New York: M. I. T. Press, 1961.

————. *The Human Use of Human Beings: Cybernetics and Society.* New York: Avon Books, Inc., 1967.

Young, Philip. *Ernest Hemingway*, revised ed. Minneapolis: University of Minnesota Press, 1965.

Zweig, Stefan. *The Living Thoughts of Tolstoy.* New York: Fawcett Publications, Inc., 1963.

B. *Articles*

Aldridge, John W. "Contemporary Fiction and Mass Culture," *New Orleans Review*, I (Fall, 1968), 4-9.

Bigsby, C. W. E. "The Impact of the 'Absurd' on American Literature," *Midcontinent American Studies Journal*, VIII (Fall, 1967), 72-79.

Bluestone, George. "John Wain and John Barth: The Angry and the Accurate." *Massachusetts Review*, I (Autumn, 1960), 582-89.

Bradbury, John M. "Absurd Insurrection: The Barth-Percy Affair," *South Atlantic Quarterly*, LXVIII (Summer, 1969), 319-29.

Bryer, Jackson. "John Barth," *Critique*, VI (Winter, 1963-64), 86-89.

Buckeye, Robert. "The Anatomy of the Psychic Novel," *Critique*, IX, ii (1967), 33-45.

Burgess, Anthony. "The Postwar American Novel: A View From the Periphery," *The American Scholar*, XXXV (Winter, 1965-66), 150-56.

Denniston, Constance. "The American Romance Parody: A Study of Purdy's *Malcolm* and Heller's *Catch-22*," *Emporia State Research Studies*, XIV, ii, 42-59, 63-64.

Dippie, Brian W. "His Visage Wild, His Form Exotic; Indian Themes and Cultural Guilt in John Barth's *The Sot-Weed Factor*," *American Quarterly*, XXI (Spring, 1969), 113-21.

Diser, Phillip E. "The Historical Ebenezer Cooke," *Critique*, X, iii (1968), 48-59.

Doskow, Minna. "The Night Journey in *Catch-22*," *Twentieth-Century Literature*, XII (Jan., 1967), 186-93.

Enck, John. "John Barth: An Interview," *Wisconsin Studies in Contemporary Literature*, VI (Winter-Spring, 1965), 3-14.

French, Michael. "The American Novels in the Sixties," *Midwest Quarterly*, IX (April 25, 1968), 365-79.

French, Warren. "The Quaking World of James Purdy," *Stetson Studies in the Humanities*, no. 1 (1963), pp. 112-22.

Galloway, David. "Clown and Saint: The Hero in Current American Fiction," *Critique*, VII (Spring-Summer, 1965), 46-65.

Golwyn, Judith. "New Creative Writers," *Library Journal*, LXXXI (June, 1956), 1496.

Gordon, Caroline and Jeanne Richardson. "Flies in Their Eyes? A Note on Joseph Heller's *Catch-22*," *Southern Review*, III (Jan., 1967), 96-105.

Green, Martin. "Science and Sensibility," *Kenyon Review*, XXV (Autumn, 1963), 699-728.

Greenberg, Alvin. "The Novel of Disintegration: Paradoxical Impossibility in Contemporary Fiction," *Wisconsin Studies in Contemporary Literature*, VII (Winter-Spring, 1966), 103-24.

Gross, Beverly. "The Anti-Novels of John Barth," *Chicago Review*, XX (Nov., 1968), 95-109.

Gurian, Jay. "Style in the Literary Desert: *Little Big Man*," *Western American Literature*, III (Winter, 1969), 285-96.

Hassan, Ihab. "Laughter in the Dark: The New Voice in American Fiction." *American Scholar*, XXXIV (Autumn, 1964), 636-40.

————. "The Novel of Outrage: A Minority Voice in Post-war American Fiction," *American Scholar*, XXXIV (Spring, 1965), 239-53.

————. "Conscience and Incongruity: The Fiction of Thomas Berger," *Critique*, V (Fall, 1962), 4-15.

————. "The Dismemberment of Orpheus: Reflections on Modern Culture, Language, and Literature," *American Scholar*, XXXII (Summer, 1963), 463-84.

Hausdorff, Don. "The Multiple Absurdities of Thomas Pynchon's *V.*," *Wisconsin Studies in Contemporary Literature*, VII (Autumn, 1966), 258-69.

Harr, Paul. "The Small, Sad World of James Purdy," *Chicago Review*, XIV (Autumn-Winter, 1960), 19-25.

Hertzel, Leo J. "What's Wrong with the Christians?" *Critique*, XI, iii (1969), 11-24. [on Coover's novels]

————. "An Interview with Robert Coover," *Critique*, XI, iii (1969), 25-29.

Hill, Hamlin. "Modern American Humor: The Janus Laugh," *College English*, XXV (Dec., 1963), 170-76.

————. "Black Humor: Its Cause and Cure," *Colorado Quarterly*, XVII (1968), 57-64.

Holder, Alan. " 'What Marvelous Plot ... Was Afoot?' History in Barth's *The Sot-Weed Factor*," *American Quarterly*, XX (Fall, 1968), 596-604.

Howe, Irving. "Mass Society and Post-Modern Fiction," *Partisan Review*, XXVI (Summer, 1959), 420-36.

Hurley, Paul. "France and America: Versions of the Absurd," *College English*, XXVI (May, 1965), 634-40.

Kaplan, Charles. "Escape into Hell: Friedman's *Stern*," *College English Journal*, I, iii (1968), 25-30.

Kern, Edith. "The Self and the Other: A Dilemma of Existential Fiction," *Comparative Literature Studies*, V (1967), 329-37.

Kiely, Benedict. "Ripeness Was Not All: John Barth's *Giles Goat-Boy*," *Hollins Critic*, III, v (1966), 1-12.

Knapp, Edgar H. "Found in the Barthhouse: Novelists as Savior," *Modern Fiction Studies*, XIV (Winter, 1968-69), 446-51.

Kostelanetz, Richard. "Dada and the Future of Fiction," *Works* (Spring, 1968), pp. 58-66.

————. "Le roman americain 'absurde,'" *Les Temps Modernes*, 21 annee, number CCXXXIV (April, 1966), 1856-66.

Krumer, Regina P. "Two Guests in Two Societies," *English Record*, XVII (April, 1967), 28-32. [on James Purdy]

Lehan, Richard. "Existentialism in Recent American Fiction: The Demonic Quest," *Texas Studies in Language and Literature*, I (Summer, 1959), 181-202.

Lehan, Richard and Jerry Patch. "*Catch-22*: The Making of a Novel," *Minnesota Review*, VII, iii (1967), 238-44.

Levine, Edward. "The Inflated Image: Satire and Meaning in Pop Art," *Satire Newsletter*, VI, i (1968), 43-50.

Levine, Paul. "The Intemperate Zone: The Climate of Contemporary American Fiction," *Massachusetts Review*, VIII (Summer, 1967), 505-23.

Loukides, Paul. "Some Notes on the Novel of the Absurd." *CEA Critic*, XXX, iv (1968), 8, 13.

Lorch, Thomas. "Purdy's *Malcolm*: A Unique Vision of Radical Emptiness," *Wisconsin Studies in Contemporary Literature*, VI (Summer, 1965), 204-13.

Longleigh, Peter J. "Donald Barthelme's *Snow White*," *Critique*, XI, iii (1969), 30-34.

MacDonald, J. L. "I See Everything Twice!: The Structure of Joseph Heller's *Catch-22*," *University Review*, XXXIV (Spring, 1968), 175-80.

McDonald, Daniel. "Science, Literature, and Absurdity," *South Atlantic Quarterly*, LXVI (Winter, 1967), 42-49.

McHenry, G. B. "Significant Corn: *Catch-22*," *The Critical Review* (Sydney-Melbourne), IX (1966), 133-44.

McNamara, Eugene. "The Post-Modern American Novel," *Queens Quarterly*, LXIX (Summer, 1962), 265-75.

————. "The Absurd Style in Contemporary American Literature," *Humanities Association Bulletin*, XIX (Spring, 1968), 44-49.

Mellard, James M. "*Catch-22*: Deja Vu and the Labyrinth of Memory," *Bucknell Review*, XVI (May, 1968), 29-44.

Miller, Russel H. "*The Sot-Weed Factor*: A Contemporary Mock-Epic," *Critique*, VIII (Winter, 1965-66), 188-200.

Monk, Samuel Holt. "The Pride of Lemuel Gulliver," *Sewanee Review*, LXIII (Winter, 1955), 54-55.

Montgomery, Marion. "The Loss of High Innocence in Our Letters: The Self and Its Aimless Quest," *Florida Quarterly*, I, iv (1968), 17-30.

Moore, Harry T. "The Present-Day American Novel," *Essays by Divers Hands*, XXXI, 123-42.

Muste, John M. "Better to Die Laughing: The War Novels of Joseph

Heller and John Ashmead," *Critique*, V (Winter, 1962-63), 16-27.

Nolland, Richard W. "John Barth and the Novel of Comic Nihilism," *Wisconsin Studies in Contemporary Literature*, VII (Autumn, 1966), 239-57.

Numasawa, Koj. "Black Humor: An American Aspect," *Studies in English Literature*, XLIV (1968), 177-93.

Pinsker, Sanford. "Heller's *Catch-22*: Protest of a *Puer Eternis*," *Critique*, VII (Winter, 1964-65), 150-62.

Poirier, Richard. "The Politics of Self-Parody," *Partisan Review*, XXXV (Spring, 1968), 339-53.

Pomeranz, Regina. "The Hell of Not Loving: Purdy's Modern Tragedy," *Renascence*, XVI (Spring, 1964), 149-53.

Rovit, Earl. "The Novel as Parody," *Critique*, VI (Winter, 1963-64), 77-85.

Rubin, Louis D. "Six Novels and S. Levin," *Sewanee Review*, LXX (July-Sept., 1962), 504-14.

Schickel, Richard. "The Floating Opera," *Critique*, VI (Winter, 1963-64), 53-67.

————. "The Old Critics and the New Novel," *Wisconsin Studies in Contemporary Literature*, V (Winter-Spring, 1964), 26-36.

Schmerl, Rudolf B. "Fantasy as Technique," *Virginia Quarterly Review*, XLIII (Autumn, 1967), 644-56.

Schultz, Max F. "Wallant and Friedman: The Glory and Agony of Love," *Critique*, X, iii (1968), 31-47.

————. "Pop, Op, and Black Humor: The Aesthetics of Anxiety," *College English*, XXX (Dec., 1968), 230-40.

Schwarzschild, Bettina. "Aunt Alma: James Purdy's *The Nephew*," *University of Windsor Review*, III (Fall 1967), 80-87.

————. "The Forsaken: James Purdy's *Malcolm*," *Texas Quarterly*, X (Spring, 1967), 170-77.

Shulman, Robert. "Myth, Mr. Eliot, and the Comic Novel," *Modern Fiction Studies*, XII (Winter, 1966-67), 395-403.

Shulman, Max. "American Humor: Its Cause and Cure," *Yale Review*, LI (Oct., 1961), 119-24.

Skerrett, Joseph Taylor, Jr. "James Purdy and the Works: Love and Tragedy in Five Novels," *Twentieth-Century Literature*, XV (April, 1969), 25-33.

Smith, Herbert. "Barth's Endless Road," *Critique*, VI (Winter, 1963-64), 68-76.

Solomon, Jan. "Structure of *Catch-22*," *Critique*, IX, ii (1967), 46-57.

Stanford, Raney. "The Romantic Hero and That Fatal Selfhood," *Centennial Review*, XII, 430-54.

Stern, J. P. "War and the Comic Muse," *Comparative Literature*, XX (Summer, 1968), 193-216.

Stubbs, John C. "John Barth as a Novelist of Ideas: The Themes of

Value and Identity," *Critique*, VIII (Winter, 1965-66), 101-16.

Sutton, Henry. "Notes Toward the Destitution of Culture," *Kenyon Review*, XXX (1968), 108-15.

Tanner, Tony. "The Hoax That Joke Bilked," *Partisan Review*, XXXIV (Winter, 1967), 102-9.

Trachtenberg, Stanley. "The Hero in Stasis," *Critique*, VII (Winter, 1964-65), 5-17.

―――. "Barth and Hawkes: Two Fabulators," *Critique*, VI (Winter, 1963-64), 4-18.

Wain, John. "A New Novel About Old Troubles," *Critical Quarterly*, V (Summer, 1963), 168-73. [on *Catch-22*]

Waldmeir, Joseph J. "Two Novelists of the Absurd: Heller and Kesey," *Wisconsin Studies in Contemporary Literature*, V (Autumn, 1964), 192-204.

Way, Brian. "Formal Experiment and Social Discontent: Joseph Heller's *Catch-22*," *Journal of American Studies*, II (Oct., 1968), 253-70.

Woodcock, George. "Utopias in Negative," *Sewanee Review*, LXIV (Winter, 1956), 85.

Wylder, Delbert E. "Thomas Berger's *Little Big Man* as Literature," *Western American Literature*, III (Winter, 1969), 273-84.

Young, James D. "The Enigma Variations of Thomas Pynchon," *Critique*, X, i (1968), 69-77.

C. *Reviews and Articles in Non-Professional Journals*

Algren, Nelson. "The Radical Innocent," *The Nation*, CXCIX (September 21, 1964), 142-43. [on Bruce Jay Friedman]

Barth, John. "The Literature of Exhaustion," *The Atlantic*, CCXX (August, 1967), 29-34.

Beatty, Jerome, Jr. "What's Happening to Humor?" *Saturday Review*, XLVII (August 29, 1964), p. 49.

Bellow, Saul. "Some Notes on Recent American Fiction," *Encounter*, XX (Nov., 1963), 122, 22-29.

"The Black Humorists," *Time*, LXXXV (February 12, 1965), 94-96.

Brustein, Robert. "Who's Killing the Novel?" *The New Republic*, CLIII (October 23, 1965), 22-24.

―――. "Logic of Survival in a Lunatic World," *The New Republic*, CXLV (November 13, 1961), 11-13. [on Catch-22]

Bryan, C. D. B. "Kurt Vonnegut: Head Bokononist," *The New York Times Book Review*, LXXIV (April 6, 1969), 2.

Davis, Douglas M. "And Up Pops the 'Pop Novel,' or Black Humor Without a Sting," *The National Observer*, April 4, 1966.

―――. "The New Mood: An Obsession with the Absurd," *The National Observer*, February 15, 1965.

―――. "Black Humor," *Freelance*, August, 1965.

Elliot, George P. "Destroyers, Defilers, and Confusers of Men," *Atlantic Monthly*, CCXXII (December 1968), 74-80.

Feiffer, Jules. "Pop-Sociology," *The New York Herald Tribune Magazine Supplement*, January 9, 1966.

Fiedler, Leslie. "Cross the Border, Close the Gap," *Playboy*, XVI (Dec., 1969), 151, 230, 252-58.

————. "John Barth: An Eccentric Genius," *The New Leader*, XLIV (February 23, 1961), 23.

Garvis, Robert. "What Happened to John Barth?" *Commentary*, XLII (Oct., 1966), 89-95.

Heller, Joseph. "*Catch-22* Revisited," *Holiday*, XLIV (April, 1967), 123-25.

"Heroic Comedy," *Newsweek*, LXVIII (August 8, 1966), 81-81B. [on • Barth]

Klein, Marcus. "Gods and Goats," *Reporter*, XXXV (September 22, 1966), 60-62. [on Barth]

Kostelanetz, Richard. "The New American Fiction," *Ramparts*, III (January-February, 1965), 57-62.

————. "The Point Is That There Isn't Any Point," *The New York Times Book Review*, LXX (June 6, 1965), 3.

Kubly, Herbert. "The Vanishing Novel," *Saturday Review*, LVII (May 2, 1964), 12-14, 26.

Morris, Robert K. "James Purdy and the Works," *Nation*, CCV (October 9, 1967), 342-44.

Murphy, Richard W. "In Print: John Barth," *Horizon*, V (Jan., 1965), 36-37.

Roth, Philip. "Writing American Fiction," *Commentary*, XXI (March, 1961), 223-33.

Rubin, Louis D., Jr. "Notes on the Literary Scene: Their Own Language," *Harpers*, CCXXX (April, 1965), 173-75.

Samuels, Charles T. "John Barth: A Buoyant Denial of Relevance," *Commonweal*, LXXXV (Oct. 21, 1966), 80-81.

Schickel, Richard. "Black Comedy with Purifying Laughter," *Harpers*, CCXXXII (May, 1966), 103. [on Vonnegut]

Schott, Webster. "James Purdy: American Dreams," *The Nation*, CXCVIII (March 23, 1964), 300-2.

Shepherd, R. Z. *Life*, LX (April 8, 1966), 15. [on Vonnegut]

Sklar, Robert. "The New Novel, USA: Thomas Pynchon," *The Nation*, CCV (September 25, 1967), 277-80.

"So They Say," *Mademoiselle*, LVII (August 1963), 234-35. [an interview with Heller]

Thurber, James. "THE FUTURE, IF ANY, OF COMEDY or, where do we non-go from here?" *Harpers*, CCXXIII (Dec., 1961), 40-45.

Index